Mortimer Collins, Edmund Yates

Thoughts in my Garden

Vol. II

Mortimer Collins, Edmund Yates

Thoughts in my Garden
Vol. II

ISBN/EAN: 9783337074821

Printed in Europe, USA, Canada, Australia, Japan

Cover: Foto ©ninafisch / pixelio.de

More available books at **www.hansebooks.com**

BY
MORTIMER COLLINS.

EDITED BY
EDMUND YATES.

WITH NOTES BY THE EDITOR AND MRS. MORTIMER COLLINS.

IN TWO VOLUMES.
VOL. II.

LONDON:
RICHARD BENTLEY AND SON,
Publishers in Ordinary to Her Majesty the Queen.
1880.

CONTENTS OF VOL. II.

CHAPTER	PAGE
I. AUTUMN, 1874	1
II. JANUARY AND FEBRUARY, 1875	49
III. SPRING, 1875	80
IV. SUMMER, 1875	135
V. 1875. JULY AND AUGUST	173
VI. AUTUMN, 1875	207
VII. 1876	258

THOUGHTS IN MY GARDEN.

CHAPTER I.

AUTUMN, 1874.

Ah, me ! for the summer that's dying,
   As summers have died heretofore !
The yachts and the swallows are flying ;
   The last man in town is a bore.
The belle of the season is married
   To some one with millions a year,
Whose brain as a desert is arid,
   Whose *terre* is petroleum or beer.
As for me, in the stern of my skiff I
   Am smoking, right cosily curl'd ;
The first breeze takes me off in a jiffy—
   Egad, 'tis the way of the world.*

---

* Written for the *World* newspaper.

Disraeli is flirting with ladies
　　In houses all à la *Lothair;*
Stern Gladstone has gone into Hades,
　　With Homer to pilot him there;
Staunch Forster is talking scholastic;
　　George Bowyer's explaining finance;
Old Roebuck is charmingly drastic;
　　Bazaine's coming hither from France.
Belfast has been bother'd by Tyndall,
　　Who wonderful epithets hurl'd,
The people of Ulster to kindle.
　　He fail'd. 'Tis the way of the world.

Now why should the leisure of autumn
　　Be broken by idiots who prate?
If fierce old Procrustes had caught 'em,
　　They'd have met with a definite fate.
The Commons are ceasing to bore us
　　With endless cabal and caprice;
So philosophers, yelling in chorus,
　　Extinguish our holiday peace.
'Gainst the Deity, perhaps, or the Bible,
　　The wiseacre's flag is unfurl'd:
And you can't bring an action for libel,
　　Ah, well! 'tis the way of the world.

But keen as the rapier of Tagus,
　　And radiant as Venus at morn,
Destroying the blockheads who plague us,
　　With an easy ineffable scorn,
The *World* in its orbit elastic
　　Moves onward, a marvellous sphere,
Its sculpture perfection of plastic,
　　Its satire serenely severe.

The idiot is flogg'd till he winces,
 The beauty with lyrics impearl'd ;
We're impartial to roughs and to princes—
 And that's the true way of the world.

Sept. 10.

If it is the dull season for newspapers, the reason is that for the world in general it is not at all dull. The men whose speeches in Parliament we read eagerly are now enjoying the Englishman's annual holiday. The brilliant leader-writers who brought literary cayenne to our breakfast-tables, are now climbing mountains or sauntering by the sea, and secondary subjects are treated by secondary hands. The beautiful girls whom the season brought to the front—delicious flowers of humanity, some tremulous as the lily of the woods, some superb as the royal rose—are all away at country seats and pleasant places, riding, rowing, playing lawn billiards and tennis, sororising with the rustic maidenhood of their parishes, rising early and going early to bed for their complexions' sake, getting refreshment after the terrible strain of London. That city is empty, in fact, though there are a few millions left in it; and we find, in our morning paper, intelligence of various murders which people seem to wait to commit till Parliament rises. It is very kind of them; though I don't care much for murder myself, and have never considered it, like De Quincey, one of the fine arts. But there are people who gloat over every hideous detail of a murder; who would rather read such vile trash than the noblest speech ever uttered by a great statesman; who would doubtless be murderers themselves, for the excitement of it, if they were not absolute, abject cowards. I wonder what percentage of murder is caused by sensational reports of murder in the newspapers. Our 'best possible public instructors' are answerable for much folly, and for a certain amount of crime.

Sept. 14.

Readers of modern French poetry will remember a classic gem of Théophile Gautier's, concerning the swallows, which I have before quoted.

We must soon lose the swallows, though

Thoughts in my Garden.

the house-marten sometimes delays till November, and, indeed, a pair are now building under my eaves, but probably will leave the nest unfinished till next year. However, the swallows are already holding their annual parliament previous to migration, only they no longer congregate *sur le toit*, as they were wont to do. Seven lines of telegraph wire are now stretched along the old Bath road, giving us in a high wind the music of a vast Æolian harp, and the giant posts which carry them look down with disdain on the neglected pumps which were used for watering the roads in the palmy days of the Royal Mail. On these wires the swallows now hold their *conciliabules*, having quite deserted the cottage roofs. I fear, from their frequent meetings, that they will soon take wing.

Sept. 17.

A correspondent of the *Times* makes a very good suggestion in reference to the prevalent grouse disease: it is, that salt should be supplied to the birds, since salt kills all parasites. Grass-feeding animals are very liable to parasites, and should always have the well-known antidote. Of grouse, I regret to say, I know very little, except on the table: but all graminivorous birds that I have observed are very fond of salt. All the birds in the neighbourhood come to peck at the salt which I throw down for my pigeons, who are clamorous for it, if any day it chances to be forgotten. Keepers of pigeons and poultry should always supply them with salt. Horses also need it. Dogs should never be allowed to touch a grain in any form.

Talking of birds, I find in last week's *Notes and Queries*, reference to a charming passage in Hurdis's 'Village Curate,' expressing admiration of bird architecture;

> 'A bird's nest! Mark it well, within, without,
> No tool had he that wrought, no knife to cut,
> No nail to fix, no bodkin to insert,
> No glue to join; his little beak was all,
> And yet how neatly finished! What nice hand,
> With every implement and means of art,
> And twenty years' apprenticeship to boot,
> Could make me such another?'

There is much more simple poetry of this sort in the works of Hurdis—Cowper's contemporary and correspondent—which this age of many books is content to forget. Hurdis was Professor of Poetry at Oxford, and died at the early age of thirty-eight.

The earliest observer and lover of birds among the poets appears to have been Aristophanes. In the "Ornitheo" he has a passage which might have suggested what I have just quoted, though of course it is infinitely more poetical. The amazement of Peisthetairos, when the messenger tells him that the new city in the sky is already built by the birds, is very fine indeed. τίνες ᾠκοδόμησαν αὐτὸ τηλικουτονί; he exclaims—and the messenger answers:

> 'The birds, no others, no Ægyptian bricklayers,
> No stonecutter or clerk of the works; they did it all;
> It seems a wonder to me. Out of Libya
> Three myriad cranes, who had swallowed the foundation stones
> Came flying; corncrakes set to work and planed them;
> A myriad storks brought up the bricks; the seagulls
> And all their ocean brotherhood brought water.'

The whole of this scene, from which I translate *currente calamo*, is full of proof that Aristophanes understood the habits of birds, even as his marvellous nightingale songs show what a subtle ear he had for their music. Shelley and Wordsworth on the skylark, and Keats on the nightingale, seem poor and tame alongside of the infinitely various bird-music of Aristophanes.

Professor Robinson Ellis, at page 14 of the preface to 'Poems of Catullus,' remarking on the attempts to render Latin verse into the same English metre, says that 'Tennyson's three specimens are, at least in English, still unique.' These specimens are of course the 'Boädicea,' the 'Alcaics on Milton,' and the hendecasyllabics, printed at the end of the volume which contains 'Enoch Arden.' Now, whatever may be said of 'Boädicea,' questionless a fine poem in the manner of 'Atys,' its metre is not the galliambus. The maximum number of syllables in a Catullian galliambus is seventeen, whereas several of Mr. Tennyson's contain twenty. But an essay on the galliambus is beyond the limits of these notes. Turning to Mr. Tennyson's second specimen, the fine 'Alcaics on Milton':

'God-gifted organ : voice of England'—

I am constrained to remark that there is a most ill-sounding false quantity in the final verse :

'Whisper in odorous heights of even.'

What saith the learned grammarian of the fourth verse in the Alcaic strophe ?—' Quartus denique habet duos dactylos cum totidem trochæis acat.' Now, is *odorous* a dactyl, either to the ear or by derivation ? Certainly not ; it is a tribrach, which might take the place of an iambus or trochee, but can by no prosodial law be substituted for a dactyl.

Sept. 24.

I observe in the *Athenæum* last week a review of a book on birds, by a Mrs. or Miss Buist. I refer to it because I like birds (and I rejoice to say that birds like me), and because the reviewer extracts from it a 'bird ghost story.' A canary died. Its mate was removed, the cage cleansed, but no bird could ever be induced to inhabit that cage. They moped and were miserable if placed in it. *The cage was haunted!* Here is a charming topic of speculation for the spiritualists. If canaries can see ghosts, verily there is no more to be said; human beings who can't see ghosts must be altogether inferior animals. But a lady to whom I showed this statement in the *Athenæum*, and who has an universal amount of what our forefathers called mother wit, at once remarked that doubtless there was dry rot in the woodwork of the cage, which probably killed the first bird, and made its successors miserable. I am disposed to think my fair friend was right, and to reject the theory of a haunted birdcage.

While I am on supernatural subjects, I may state that recently I have had some converse with a gentleman who professes to have regular intercourse with the realm of spirits. He is so thoroughly in earnest that I cannot laugh at him; and, as he is both a scholar and a man of business, how can I question his sanity? He told me the other day that he had a vision of the mansion I am to occupy in the next world. The front door opens on a great market-place; the back door on solitary silent woods; and between those doors a stream of water flows—which I hope won't make the house damp. The flowers in the garden are chiefly purple, which colour, he says, is connected with me, though I certainly am not *porphyrogenitus.* What makes men conjure up these delusions? I, for my part, am willing to wait and see, in the due time of revelation, what is to be my fate. The conscience of man (which is the faculty that connects the single soul with the Infinite soul) should make him brave and incurious. Doing that which is right, you grasp the hand of the Allfather, and that grasp gives safety. What manner of habitation is prepared for you hereafter may be left to those who have souls for upholstery.

※ ※ ※ ※ ※

There has been a Congress of fungologists or mycophagists at Aberdeen. I like mushrooms. I agree with Martial:

'Argentum atque aurum facile est, lanamque, togamque,
    Mittere: boletos mittere difficile est.'

Also the truffle is a grand tuber, and goes well in pie of goose-liver or of game. But it seems that the sparassis, which is just like macaroni, has now been found in England: and 'among the edible fungi was an enormous specimen of the *lycoperdon giganteum* [the *Times* misprints it *hycoperdon*] which had been gathered at Fetternear, in the North of Scotland.' The lycoperdon is excellent cut in slices and fried in Lucca oil—while, if powdered and submitted to heat, its fumes have an effect like that of chloroform. I should like to see an open exhibition of edible fungi where poor people could learn their value. They are among the most nutritious forms of food, but myriads of mushrooms, morels, truffles, chantarelles, champignons, are wasted every year because the poor do not understand their use. I was once picking mushrooms on a common when a tramp piteously told me he had eaten nothing but blackberries for two days. When I recommended him to imitate me, and eat some mushrooms, he evidently thought I was laughing at him.

Oct. 1.

The other day a lady lent me the *Cornhill Magazine*. There are two stories going in it, both what is called in our vile slang 'sensational'—that is, morbid and prurient. In the heart of the silliest of the two (which were the only articles cut open in the number) I found a tract! It is called 'The Stone-Breaker,' and published at Paternoster Row, No. 19, and at the Bazaar, Soho Square. It amused me to think that the person who meant to distribute this tract was solacing herself meanwhile with a prurient novel. And then I thought of my old friend Jack Templar, whom I have not seen for many a year. We were, about the time of the Crimean War, dining at the 'Cock.' He insisted on some of that rare old port which I fear has been drunken out long ago. 'Ah, Jack,' said one of us, 'you're flush of money just now. That *Quarterly* article on Catullus brought you coin, old fellow. And then those capital translations from Heine, in *Blackwood*.'

'Pooh!' says Jack Templar, 'those things won't find you oysters for your steak. I do them just to keep my hand in. My income is from *tracts*. I have just got a sum I won't name, lest some of you fellows should propose a loan, for a tract called "The Saint in the Scullery." Murray and Blackwood are all very well, but the tract societies are the beggars to pay. Now, waiter, some more of old Tennyson's port.'

I don't know whether Jack still writes tracts; he certainly did not write 'The Stone-Breaker,' as there's a blunder in it (p. 4) about 'publicans' which my classical friend could not have made. Doubtless his tracts did good in their time. Such a class of literature being inevitable, the better it is done the less injurious it will be.

Oct. 8.

If my notes are dull and brief this day, kind-hearted readers will forgive me when I tell them that I have just put turf on the tomb of a favourite Skye terrier, who died suddenly on Wednesday. He was the most affectionate, irritable, excitable dog in the world; would bite my boot savagely if by accident, I touched him, and then put his cool black nose in my hand by way of apology. He was given me eight years ago by the editor of one of our Quarterlies, because in his jealous moods he *would* bite the legs of a newly-arrived editorial baby. It is a Liberal review, so I at once accepted Fido as a Tory dog. Tory he was, to the backbone. He loved his mistress and he hated cats. Can a good Constitutional dog's epitaph be written in fewer words? Well, he was skylarking in my bookroom with his heels in the air; and then he rushed out on the lawn in the sunshine; and then we heard a strange scream—and dear old Fido was picked up dead. I suppose it is humiliating to confess that I have shed some tears about him. If my aunt, Miss Angelina Vixen, had died and left me that quiet two thousand a year on which she now maintains missionaries and cats, I might not have wept much; but I did mourn my poor dear irrepressible troublesome Fi, who was wont to interrupt me in the midst of an attempted epigram. With my own hands have I buried my dear friend beneath the yellowing limes. Shall I meet his spirit again? Ah! who can solve that problem?

Oct. 15.

James Dobson of Bath usually calls to see me once a year. He called the other day; and, as the sky was rainy and the weather 'juicy,' he deigned to accept a glass of whisky—the best of spirits, as is well known in Caledonia (stern and wild, fit nurse for a poetic child), for keeping the damp out of a man who is deerstalking or grouse-shooting, or (far humbler occupation) selling birds to all buyers. This last doth James Dobson of Bath; and in his glass-shielded cart carries about a good many pounds' worth of rare birds which he offers to all who like 'the angels of the air.' Real beauties are they, charming vagaries of nature; but I introduced James Dobson to a couple of tame owls, taken in the woods close by, and comfortably housed on my back lawn, that rather astonished him. The exoteric wisdom of the owl is wonderful;

he beats Lord Thurlow. Talking of birds, my most familiar robin insists on taking a matutinal stroll with me: I hear his voice in the hedge or on the telegraph wires that dominate the road, and there he is, singing a morning welcome. And the young thrushes are learning their mellow music of delicious repetition now: I hear them as I lie lazily in bed, wondering when my bath water will come up, and what in the world I shall write about. Day after day they have improved; it was a prattling song first, like a baby's: now I will back one young mavis in my trees against the Patti herself. Thank God for the birds!

Oct. 22.

Some one has kindly sent me a copy of the *Rock*, with a fierce review of a High Church confessional manual. The *Rock* is Evangelical. I admit that such a journal may be necessary to fight the periodicals with Papist proclivities; but I really should like to see a higher and more independent tone. Πάντες οἱ λαβόντες μάχαιραν ἐν μαχαίρᾳ ἀπολοῦνται. Let us have a sober and serene strength in our theologic discussion. The *Rock* is angry about a manual privately printed for the use of clergy who encourage confession. I should be angrier than the *Rock* if I were not sure that the father confessor is a fool, and would be a fool in any condition of life, and that the women he subjects to obscene questioning and discipline are women devoid of real moral and intellectual power. English ladies do not deign to listen to these fellows; their field lies among persons of a low type, imperfectly educated. It is easy to guess what results may arrive where the confessing priest encounters the confiding minx. In England ladies are healthful and wise, and their brothers wear heavy boots, and the morbid curate has to lure persons of the lower middle-class to his confessional. Pity that a policeman cannot always be on duty there!

Oct. 27.

How does the Mendicity Society propose to deal with that great plague, the licensed hawker, whose license now costs so little that these half-mendicants have pestilently increased? The women are the worst and the most numerous. My gate is just opposite telegraph post No. 565 on the old Bath road; few days pass without visitors of this kind. They bring trashy lace, sham jewellery, pots and pans, cheap stationery; sometimes they go to the back door and try to cajole the maids; sometimes (especially if it is a fine day and you are sitting or strolling on your lawn) they come right in at the front with their vile trash, and almost insist on your buying. I have been told by one of these impudent wenches that she had the Queen's license, and had as much right in my garden as I had; indeed, she threatened me with a summons because my dog barked at her. Can the Mendicity Society suggest some way of dealing with this pest?

Oct. 29.

What weather! Will the meteorologists explain it? I am writing now with windows wide open; and, but that I see before me ripening medlars, a Canadian oak turning scarlet, a chestnut green and gold, a boy sweeping up innumerable lime-leaves, I should fancy it was the middle of July. When we get a chilly autumn it is ascribed to wandering icebergs. Is this delicious October warmth due to a volcano or a coming comet?

※ ※ ※ ※ ※

The book of the week is the 'Greville Memoirs,' and I observe that some journal states that its editor, Mr. Henry Reeve, has increased his literary reputation by the way in which he has produced it. I fearlessly say that it is a book no gentleman could write. Greville, Clerk of the Council in the reigns of George IV. and William IV., was a spy and a snob. No language is too strong to use about such a fellow. You would horsewhip your servant for conduct like his. He calls King William IV. a blackguard and a buffoon; he may be right, but is it the way in which a servant should write of his master? Greville's diary will be read freely enough; people like such gossip; but the extracts I have seen from it show that he was a very vulgar *valet,* who took delight in chronicling the weaknesses of kings and queens. Such contemptible persons have their use in the world, doubtless; but it is a great pity that our foremost critical journals do not exactly indicate their actual position. It has been written of George IV.:

> 'A noble, nasty race he ran,
> Supremely filthy and fastidious;
> He was the world's first gentleman,
> And made the appellation hideous.'

Yet was he a man of nearer approach to manliness than the spying, chattering Greville, his Clerk of the Council. And had George IV. known what a spy and traitor Greville was, he would have dismissed him from his employment.

Nov. 2.

I was the other day chatting with an eminent *librarius*, who is not without poetical and critical capacity. Our theme was the modern novel—that form of literature which might be a very noble thing, and is for the most part a very mean thing. To him, the vast demand for novels is a nuisance; the trashiest books must be bought, for a circulating library must contain whatsoever is asked for. But my friend holds that the plague of novels is curing itself by its own excess. So many 'fools rush in' to the field of fiction that the true angels of genius tread in other tracks. Again the public taste improves, and novels of seduction and bigamy are less read by far; and the worst offenders in sensation find they must cultivate a quieter style. This is satisfactory, so far as it goes; but I cannot believe that people who began by caricaturing humanity can ever end by drawing it truly.

My observant friend tells me that he can guess from the faces and manners and dresses of the ladies who frequent his library what class of books they mean to ask for. Mr. Du Maurier could expand this charmingly into a sketch for *Punch*. How well he could mark the distinction between the lady who comes for Miss Broughton and Ouida, the lady who comes for Blackmore and—well, is there any other to be named with him?—the lady who comes for Huxley and Tyndall. There are two or three other obvious types. I wish our most admirable society sketcher would try the theme.

My colloquist is also of opinion that novel-reading closely resembles spirit-drinking; it gives a temporary excitement, which can only be kept up by more frequent and stronger doses, and which will certainly do permanent harm, shortening the life of the brain. Holding this opinion, he ought, perhaps, to shut up shop; but be it remembered that there are lawyers who think law a mistake, and doctors who take no physic, and licensed victuallers who drink no alcohol, and authors of whom it may be said (to quote an epigram some twenty years old):

> 'If by their works we judge their creed,
> 'Tis—those who write should never read.'

However, his assertion is too sweeping; wide the difference between the sound old wine of Scott and the turpentine gin manufactured by our present race of female novelists, and of men (worse still) who to please the public try to imitate the prurience of the women.

Now, I lay it down as a primary canon of

novel-writing that the hero must be a gentleman and the heroine a lady (I mean in the sense of character, not accident), and that the chief persons in the book should be persons it is pleasant to remember. There must be villains and wicked wenches in fiction, if fiction is to reflect life ; but they ought not to fill the foreground and nauseate the palate—and this is the gross blunder of modern novel-writing. When Thackeray (who borrowed his best characters from French novels) constituted Becky Sharp on the model of Dumas' 'Miladi,' he set an example which has set weaker people at work depicting scores of scamps and myriads of minxes, all of one polluted type. Yet Thackeray thought Fielding the greatest of novelists. Look at 'Tom Jones.' Tom Jones is a thorough gentleman, with all his wildness ; Sophy Western is a lovely lady ; Squire Allworthy is a noble Englishman. These three you remember, they are your friends for ever ; while Blifil, and Square, and Thwackum, and the other inferior characters, are mere shadows. Apply this test

Thoughts in my Garden. 25

to any modern novel you have read; find in it three characters, or two, or even one, that you would rather not forget—that it is a delight to think of as real. Dickens and Thackeray often stand the test well; nobody would like to lose Pickwick or Sam Weller, Warrington or Colonel Newcome. But try the test on the two or three hundred novels of the year 1874 . . . . you who read them.

* * * * *

The art of advertising is something marvellous. We all remember the hapless fate of Mr. William Stickers, who had stolen a sheep 'down to Zummerzetzhire,' and who, running off to London, beheld on the first palings he saw:

'BILL STICKERS! BEWARE!'

What could poor William Stickers do, except give himself up to the first policeman he saw (astonishing that not-easily-astonished official), and confess the unlawful mutton. Some of the notices we see on hoardings are as unintelligible to the ordinary by-passer as was this to William Stickers of Wincanton. Yet one thing is certain—the bill-sticker's art prevails. 'Tis an old proverb that, if you throw mud enough, some will stick; it may be said that, if you stick bills enough, some will pay. Fools abound. By enormous advertising the reputation of anything can be made, from a quack's pill to an idiot's epic. Will the Committee of the Stock Exchange grant a settling-day to the Bill Sticker's Company, unlimited, capital a trillion miles of coarse paper, and a quadrillion quarts of printer's ink and paste? The sooner the better; the walls of London are not yet quite hideous enough with the scabies of bounce to justify a German invasion on æsthetic grounds.

Nov. 12.

Living in town and living in the country are two widely different things; after trying both for near half a century, I confess a preference for the country. Much may be said in favour of town. You can get oysters at a moment's notice. If you are short of wine (not being a millionaire—for would, or could, any millionaire write these notes?) you may round the first corner get a bottle of Chablis or Montrachet to digest your oysters. It is quite otherwise in the country, unless, of course, you have a large establishment. I who have a cottage the size of a doll's house, with a lawn as big as a girl's pinafore, find difficulties of commissariat. I get all my meat from London, finding that the greater expense is more than balanced by quality. The lord of the manor sends me game; and I take this opportunity of remarking that any constant reader of my notes will not meet with ingratitude if he follows Sir Gilbert's example.* And in the country you get *good neighbourhood*. There is nothing of this sort in London. Your friends are scattered over a vast space with wide distances. When, after a hard night's work (it is midnight now, and I dare say the goose-quill has three hours more to do), I go down to my gate, there is a matutinal greeting from a familiar robin, and there is pretty sure to be

* M. C. experienced much kindness from Sir Gilbert Clayton East, the lord of the manor.—F. C.

somebody passing who has an original remark to make on the state of the weather; and then the friendly cottagers, just after harvest, bring me home-made bread, the product of their leasing in the wide wheat fields, better than anybody can make on scientific principles. The chief objection to a village is the gossip. Well, is there no gossip in London? Here, in my village, after long experience, I have come to the conclusion that gossip depends wholly on the parson and his wife. If the parson and the parson's wife decline to listen to gossip and to carry it into higher quarters, scandal does not live. Young curates often blunder so terribly in such matters, that one regrets they cannot be kept in order by sensible churchwardens, with power to use the birch rod for extreme silliness. But I suppose the sensible churchwarden is difficult to discover.

※　　※　　※　　※　　※

Sir John Lubbock has recently been laughing at the notion that 'every English gentleman reads Horace.' Perhaps they don't. Perhaps there are people who get up their apposite quotations, in and out of Parliament, and whose knowledge of the dear old Venusian is slightly a sham. Of course we all remember Byron ('Childe Harold's Pilgrimage,' iv. 77):

> 'Then farewell Horace; whom I hated so,
> Not for thy faults, but mine.'

As was often the case, Byron was wrong: neither Horace nor he was in fault: his tutor could not show him what the poet was driving at. I think more of us know him by heart and read him daily than Sir John Lubbock would imagine. He is not my favourite Latin poet: I prefer Catullus out and out, and like Virgil almost, if not quite, as well. But he is the man who, if born to-day, would be an Englishman pure and simple. A friend of mine says that the Sermon on the Mount is far finer in English than it ever was in Greek. I say that Horace, though quite untranslatable into English, is more English in his ideas than most Englishmen. Odd!

Mr. Ruskin, it appears, would like to be his own Boswell. I gather this from an account given of his 'Fors Clavigera' in the *Saturday*

Review. Now, why is *Fors, Clavigera?* Which does Chance carry, a club or a key? Ovid gives us Hercules *Claviger* and Janus *Claviger;* and here it is obvious which is *Clavus,* which *Clava.* But perchance our 'Oxford Graduate' is thinking of the *Laconica Clavis,* or of the *Adultera Clavis,* Shall we render *Fors Clavigera* 'the *Chance Door-key'?* It was not unknown in Rome.

To return to Ruskin: 'There is a charming passage about his travels through England with his father, the books he used to read, the pictures he used to see, and how early he discovered the political truth that it was better to live in a small house and have Warwick Castle to be astonished at, than to live in Warwick Castle and have nothing to be astonished at.' Mr. Ruskin is untrue to himself to write in such a way. I, a boy, read 'Modern Painters' before I left school, and learnt from it that there was more to astonish me in one of God's sunsets than in all the castles man ever built. And if I lived in Warwick Castle I should never want something 'to be astonished at.' Look down from its windows upon Shakespeare's Avon below! That stream, with the broken bridge Sir Launcelot may have crossed, is worth a hundred Warwick Castles—though Warwick is the second unruined castle in England.

Nov. 26.

A literary friend of mine remarked to me one day, a good many years ago, that chess is a game below the notice of men of letters. He might just as well say the same of whist. The two games have real *raisons d'être*, and I would guarantee to fathom the character of any man or woman with whom I played either. To play chess with a pretty girl is one of the nicest things in the world, and reveals her character to you marvellously. Whist with an old gentleman, whether as partner or antagonist, is a fine test of mind. There are those who laugh at games of skill and chance. I do not. They are the natural outcome of humanity. Charles Fox used to say that the most delightful thing in the world was to win at cards, and the next in the order of delight to lose. This is the exaggeration of such matters. But quite certain is it that these things indicate peculiarities of human life which would not come out in any other way. You can read character remarkably well at chess, or whist, or *écarté*.

❊ ❊ ❊ ❊ ❊

Modern literature is, I imagine, chiefly of value to the contemporary paper-maker. To put it tersely, genius facilitates the metamorphosis of rags. It is well that rags should undergo a sublimating metamorphosis. The worn-out shirt passes through the paper-mill, and comes into the hand of genius, and a poem is written upon it. Seldom, I imagine, do the ladies who write dainty notes on the creamiest paper think that the material on which they place their pleasantries was, not long ago, the shirt of a cadger, or the smock of a female tramp. If the paper on which we write could tell its story, what a story it would have to tell! An imaginative writer might make a perfect romance out of a sheet of note-paper, traced from its cradle to its

Thoughts in my Garden.

grave. But what I thought of in this connexion was the curious way in which literature and paper are connected. To use an electric simile, the author is at the positive pole; he has mind. The paper-maker is at the negative pole; he has money. Between these stand the printer, the publisher, the retailer, all of whom get far more out of a book than the author himself ever does, unless he chances to have a friend who is a good man of business. My experience (and I have published a good many books) is that the paper-maker gets most out of a book, and the author the least—a curious illustration of the comparative value of mind and matter. Perchance the balance may be rectified in the next world. Perchance the author who has to live in a cottage and drink the cheapest wines is not even in this world much less happy than the paper-maker, whose mansion includes a billiard-room and a private theatre.

* * * * *

Winter has set in rather seriously. A day or two ago we rescued a robin from death by frost, giving him shelter for the night in the kitchen, under a wire meat-cover. The poor little fellow was nearly gone, lying on his back on the grass with his legs stiff and stark. Curious what legends cling round the robin.

'Who killed Cock Robin?'

is perhaps the most popular of all nursery rhymes. Then there's the pretty story of the 'Babes in the Wood,' which that rascal Tom Ingoldsby burlesqued most wickedly, winding up with this stern stanza against cruel uncles and thievish executors:

> 'Be sure he who does such base things
>   Will never stifle Conscience's clamour;
> His "riches will make themselves wings,"
>   And his property come to the hammer.
> Then *he*—and not those he bereaves—
>   Will have most cause for sighings and sobbings,
> When he finds himself smothered with leaves
>   (Of fat catalogues) heaped up by Robins.'

In those times, when George Robins was *the* auctioneer, the pun was an epigram. But the curious, familiar kindness which seems to link the redbreast with humanity ought not to be travestied. I suppose there is no one who has lived in the country who has not made pleasant acquaintance with a robin. The quaint mediæval legend that the red on the robins' breasts came when they tried with feeble beaks to pull the nails from the hands and feet of Christ, shows how fond our ancestors were of them. In those old days things divine and human were closely mingled, and a poetic halo environed the verities of religion. Myths grew up around the imperishable truths without injuring them.

* * * * *

To what extent is modern Spiritualism (which is the merest Materialism) likely to go? When I was a boy—

> 'Ah, woeful when!
> Ah me, the change 'twixt now and then!'

says Coleridge; but, despite the authority of the great poet, I would rather be a man than a boy—but, to resume, when I was a boy, Mesmerism was the favourite folly. Several famous mesmerists tried to operate on me, but failed entirely; whereas I found that I could mesmerise almost anybody, but more especially the young ladies. Being a philosopher even at that early date, I drew my own inferences. They were that the whole thing is a mere product of excitement, half imaginative, half sensitive. It also presents an excellent mode of flirtation, under the guise of sham science. The modern spiritualists seem to me not half so amusing. To sit in a dark room and hear an accordion play in the air and be occasionally touched by a flabby hand seems to me far less amusing than to look into a pretty girl's eyes and mesmerise her, or to let her do the same to you. And when in the world are these spiritualists going to give us some ideas from the higher sphere? I have a volume of poetry somewhere, by a spiritualist of the first force, all communicated by poetical spirits, and I certainly never read such rubbish in my life. If the Spiritualist creed be true, we are all going rapidly down-hill—a *facilis descensus Averno.*

Dec. 3.

I dwell in a parish far remote from School

Boards. It is, perhaps, absurd that one parish should have its School Board and the next none at all; but our astute legislators seem to think it all right, and as I have no children to be dragged to school it matters not to me. I may note, however, two points which appear to me, from frequent observation, unwisely neglected in my village school. To some minds they may seem trifles. For aught I know, the bucolic youth may be well instructed in Greek and Latin, and algebra, but the boys who leave the school have clearly never been drilled, for they walk with a slouch that is hideous to behold, and the girls have scarcely an elementary idea of needlework. It is in these days hardly possible to find a village girl who can deftly use the needle. People may laugh at the old-fashioned samplers that our grandmothers and aunts used to work, but they were diplomas in the college of which Arachne is lady-president. Let the man who despises needlework wait till he loses a shirt-button and finds no fairy fingers to replace it.

As to drill, it would certainly do the rustic

youth a world of good. They do not even know how to walk. Their arms are a trouble to them. Their heads hang down on their shoulders as if their necks were made of india-rubber. I believe the reason why country girls often get fascinated by soldiers is not so much the scarlet coat as the fact that a soldier looks like a man. The ordinary rustic has never stood upright in his life; and if he gets into a row, and has to use his fists, he hits in a roundabout fashion. The popular tendency to put down athletic trials of skill and strength has something to do with this. The wrestlers of Cumberland and Westmerland still keep up their fine hardy sport; but I fear it is decadent in Devon and Cornwall, where Abraham Cann and Polkinghorne were once famous. Berkshire used to be great for its back-sword play, but that seems also in desuetude. Of the various instructors of my youth I think I am most grateful to my drill-master, a retired sergeant-major of the Guards, who taught us single-stick and fencing, both grand exercises. How the foils quicken the eye and strengthen the wrist! How the play of the basket-hilted sapling enlarges the lungs and steadies the nerves! But I suppose if a drill-master were to draw blood from a boy's skull in the course of a lesson in these days he would be brought before a magistrate for an assault.

Dec. 10.

Many men would, with Mr. Walter, commend Bacon to young students. I suppose it is vain to protest against the common error of calling him Lord Bacon, a title which he never held.* I must, however, protest against quoting against him Pope's phrase, 'the meanest of mankind.' Pope himself, who in a foul and cowardly way libelled ladies, suppressing his slander for a bribe, far better deserved the epithet. It is not denied that Bacon was sullied by the *vitia temporis;* but he erred from carelessness, and would not have been persecuted but that his eminent genius made him the mark of envy. The king himself, a

---

* He was Lord Verulam. That most careful writer, Isaac Disraeli, in his 'Curiosities of Literature,' makes this mistake.—F. C.

weak dabbler in literature, of whom his famous tutor said that he tried to make him a scholar and could only develop a pedant, felt a pigmy beside Bacon's intellectual grandeur. If Mr. Walter will read Mr. Spedding's 'Life of Bacon' (the noblest of modern biographies, which every man should buy who can afford the supreme luxury of a great library), he will alter his opinion on that point.

One more remark. Mr. Walter quotes, with apparent approval, the words put by a poet into the mouth of Stradivarius of Cremona:

' 'Tis God gives skill,
But not without men's hands ; God could not make
Antonio Stradivari's violin
Without Antonio.'

Now, these words, appropriate enough when ascribed by a dramatic poet to the violin-maker, involve an error against which Mr. Walter might fitly have warned his young hearers. Once grant that God *could* not make any part of His universe except in a certain way, and the true conception of the Divinity is gone. You are landed either in a Jove who is controlled by the Fates, or in one of the various theories of development which, if they admit the existence of a God at all, make Him identical with light, or heat, or the electric force, or something in the same category. The poet conceived Stradivarius as a man whose whole aim in life was to make the most perfect instrument of music, and who, feeling an inspiration thereto, believed that he only could do it. This, a true poetic conception of individual thought, should not have been presented to these youths of the Quebec Institute as philosophic truth. The Homeric 'Hymn to Hermes' is more sound, when it attributes to a god the construction of music's first instrument.

Dec. 17.

I was amused the other day by a story of a necklace—not Queen Marie Antoinette's famous necklace of diamonds—but a circlet of glass beads worn by a village schoolgirl. The mistress insisted on her taking it off; necklaces were strictly prohibited by the vicar. The girl's mother maintained her right to adorn her just as she pleased. The vicar kept to his point, and wouldn't permit anybody in a glass necklace to enter the school. The mother threatened to summon him before the magistrates, and said he had no jurisdiction over her, because she was one of 'the Brethren'—what Brethren I know not. At this the vicar collapsed, and the girl, whose mother is a Brother, wears the glass beads defiantly. What would a School Board say to this sort of thing?

The other day there were preparations for a Penny Reading with musical illustrations in a village I wot of. Among the music, portions of Coleridge's 'Ancient Mariner' were to be sung, to whose music I did not hear. That weird and mystic ballad rises above the region of music. I was surprised to encounter a clerical young gentleman there who had evidently never heard of Coleridge, the famous defender of Church and State principles, and who thought these extracts from his immortal poem 'queer sort of stuff.' I can well imagine it.* We are

* This was the young gentleman who set himself the task of reforming the village of Knowl Hill in general, and Mortimer Collins in particular.—F. C.

a prosy generation just now. It requires a poetic brain to understand the beauty of a verse like this—

> 'The fair breeze blew, the white foam flew,
>   The furrow followed free :
> We were the first that ever burst
>   Into that silent sea.'

Or—

> 'Day after day, day after day,
>   We stuck, nor breath nor motion,
> As idle as a painted ship
>   Upon a painted ocean.'

Or—

> 'Water, water, everywhere,
>   And all the boards did shrink ;
> Water, water, everywhere,
>   Nor any drop to drink.'

Or—

> 'It ceased : yet still the sails made on
>   A pleasant noise till noon,
> A noise like of a hidden brook,
>   In the leafy month of June,
> That to the sleeping woods all night
>   Singeth a quiet tune.'

Or—

> 'He prayeth best who loveth best
>   All things both great and small,
> For the dear God who loveth us
>   He made and loveth all.'

Strange it is that the purest, highest, simplest poetry is not understanded by minds of a common order. The 'Ancient Mariner' is unique; and yet there are young gentlemen of culture who regard it as ' queer sort of stuff.'

※ ※ ※ ※ ※

One thing as to Spiritualist manifestations is the fact that nothing at all inexplicable happens if only one person is present who comes to inquire and investigate. I have tried the experiment many times with private friends of my own who are not at all qualified for Hanwell, yet who can make their tables and chairs do anything when I am away. I am a kill-joy; when I appear the ghosts grow sulky. As to making a dining-table dance, why the flightiest little hussy of a lady's work-table wouldn't condescend to pirouette in my presence. Are we infidels never to have a chance of conversion?

The argument of probability in reference to Spiritualism is clear against it. If the soul be immortal, as the spiritualist admits, it will go on growing elsewhere as it has grown on earth. As Tennyson wrote of Wellington:

'There must be other nobler work to do
Than when he fought at Waterloo.'

The instinctive ambition of man is a prophecy of his future: which among us would like to think of an eternity of just the very work we are doing now? I can imagine Mr. Disraeli glad to get beyond the region of politics; Dr. Colenso rather weary of finding inaccuracies in the Pentateuch; the Poet Laureate anxious to meet a hero other than King Arthur; and, indeed, scores of people that I know who would be glad to dismount from their hobbies. But these Spiritualists, when they profess to bring back some gossiping ghost to revisit the glimpses of the gaslight, present us with an imbecile creature who has gone backward instead of forward. Worse than a Bourbon, if Shakespeare or Milton be called to the front, he has learnt nothing and forgotten everything. An invisible Shakespeare without wisdom or wit, or rhythm or rhyme, painfully hammering out nonsense on a table, is enough to make one dread immortality. Fancy, after escaping into the illimitable ether, and being winged for flights into infinitude, a recall to a dull room in a London house, to be questioned on trifles through a psychic!

Dec. 24.

Some cursory remarks of mine on matters Spiritualistic have brought me a little correspondence. Before noting it, I may observe that there is a tendency to call things by names which convey exactly the opposite meaning. There are among us, for example, scientific gentlemen who style themselves Positivists, but who are actually Negativists, since they deny the existence of any positive power to guide the universe. Similarly the persons who call themselves Spiritualists are really Materialists, their desire being to give substantial form to that impalpable essence which is the spirit of man. They cannot believe in the soul's immortality unless souls will come back and lift dining-tables and play accordions in the dark. Any sane man would prefer annihilation to an immortality of subjugation to the will of a medium.

Dec. 31.

In weather which seems to freeze the brain itself, Arctic weather of the keenest kind, it is not altogether easy to write. I am just now reminded of Keats's most Shakespearian line,

'The owl, with all his feathers, was a-cold,'

by a pair of owls caged opposite my dining-room window, that just pass all their time (except dinner-time) in the snug box provided for them. The cock turns out at about noon to look at the weather; shakes his sagacious head; returns to inform his spouse that she had better stay where she is. Lucky birds! they get fed regularly, and haven't to write books or articles to pay their bills.

This weather is making the birds eager for every crumb of bread we can spare them. We should feed them now, lest the groves should be songless in summer. My latest visitors have been a pair of ravens, that have come down to my doors in search of food. Vast birds they look in my leafless trees, with their long beaks and bright eyes. I hope no bucolic lout with unlicensed gun will shoot them down. The birds, eager for food and weak on the wing, are just now at a terrible disadvantage.

CHAPTER II.

JANUARY AND FEBRUARY, 1875.

How curiously our fancies vary
Betwixt July and January!
In Summer, little lady mine,
I twined your hair with eglantine,
In Winter, as, of course, you know,
Nought so becomes as mistletoe.

In Winter Cupid's favourite shop is
The drawing-room. and not the coppice :
Your slippered foot adorns the carpet,
Each eye is like an azure star, pet,
And the white hand that pours the Hyson,
By Aphrodite ! '*tis* a nice 'un.

Forgetting Summer's golden splendour,
Let's sit with feet upon the fender :

Let's put the skylark on his mettle,
With singing of our silver kettle,
Laugh at the follies of this clever age,
And brew our *Punch*—all-year-round beverage !*

Jan. 2.

METEOROLOGICAL prophets kindly assure us that we are to have altogether eight weeks of this terribly cold weather, which seems to paralyse the brain—to freeze it into a tiny particle somewhere in the occiput—just as the mercury shrinks into the bulb of the thermometer. For my part, I hope the meteorologists are all wrong, and that we shall have a thaw before these lines are in print. Snow is picturesque enough for a while, but one tires of it. It is all very well for the man who has leisure to skate, or to drive a sleigh with a pair of fiery horses a dozen miles an hour; but when you have to sit down and think how you may amuse the public, you naturally wish for warmer weather. Milton declared that he could write with satisfaction only between the vernal and autumnal equinoxes, and we certainly sympathise with him.

※ ※ ※ ※ ※

° Written for *Punch*.

When Mr. Greville writes of George IV. as a 'contemptible, cowardly, selfish, unfeeling dog,' the present members of the Royal Family may well be doubtful as to what sort of diaries Court officials are keeping about them. It is by no means pleasant for a Prince to feel that the highly-refined person who bows to him with every symptom of courtesy is making objectionable memoranda about him at every spare moment, wherewith to amuse the public in years to come—is even getting information about him from his body-servant. I wonder what the present able and accomplished Clerk of the Council thinks of his predecessor's conduct?

Talking of that gentleman, I think in his last work, 'Social Pressure,' his love for short proverb-like sentences has led him into a good many errors. I do not object to such a statement as that 'riches bring suspiciousness as surely as over-eating brings gout,' though perhaps it is rather too general; it ought to be limited to persons who either acquire riches for themselves or inherit them from some one who has recently acquired them. A man of a family that has been wealthy for generations is no more likely to be suspicious than the descendant of a line of able men is likely to be vain. Sir Arthur again says that 'the tendency of modern social life is to knock the brains out of society.' That I entirely deny. Everybody who knows anything of the chief coteries of really choice society, whether political or literary or artistic, is quite aware that intellect holds its own as firmly as ever it did. We have quite as good talkers as Macaulay or Rogers or Sydney Smith; and as to the ladies, I think their conversation is better than ever it was. The thing that makes certain cliques uncommonly dull is the mania for science and controversial theology which has recently appeared among us, thanks to the activity of certain lecturers and pamphleteers. This is merely a cursory movement of fashion. It is impossible permanently to interest one's self in protoplasm, or the transit of Venus, or the delicate distinctions between the actual value of Papal infallibility before and after the Vatican utterance. Even now, when the poly-

Thoughts in my Garden.   53

syllables of popular science and transcendental Catholicism are familiar to loquacious lips, you will commonly discover that the wit and the beauty at dinner-table or in drawing-room have found quite other themes. No, I cannot accept this paradox from Sir Arthur Helps.

Nor the following: 'The philosophers of each age are equally foolish; the common people gradually increase in wisdom.' What is the precise meaning of this charge of folly against the philosophers? Does Sir Arthur Helps suppose that because a philosopher sometimes amazes the public by an impossible proposal—as Plato in his 'Republic,' or Sir Thomas More in the 'Utopia,'—that therefore they hold literally to the theories they propound? Why, he must be like the Irish bishop mentioned by Swift, who said that he had read 'Gulliver's Travels,' and thought there were several things in them not quite true. As to the common people's increasing in wisdom, I only wish it were true. But all students of humanity know well that such growth is impossible. Mr. Odger is neither wiser nor more foolish than Thersites. The mob of to-day is no wiser than the mob of a hundred or a thousand years ago. They are still, as they always must be, an unreasoning race, whose passions and wants guide them, and who will follow any leader who has electric power. Are the deluded followers of Mrs. Girling any wiser than those who believed in Joanna Southcott? Are the Spiritualists wiser than the Mesmerists of the commencement of the century— or than the witches who swallowed intoxicating drugs, and dreamt that they rode on broomsticks and were introduced to Satan? When a medium asserts that she has a tame spirit who comes at her call, how far wiser is she than the old witch who firmly believed her black cat to be a familiar friend? The short, sharp sayings to which Sir Arthur Helps' is so much addicted are easily manufactured, if you don't care whether they are true or not.

Jan. 6.

The frost, which seemed to condense one's very brain, has suddenly departed, and our frolic friend Mr. *Punch's* illustrations are already reminiscences of the past. Does not everybody rejoice? A few more degrees of cold is killing to the weak; it was pitiful to see the number of old people whose deaths were recorded day after day in the obituary of the *Times*. The sudden thaw has filled the brooks and ponds with water; and those who know the difficulties which come on agriculturists by reason of want of water in the heat of summer are amazed at the shortsightedness which makes no attempt at storage. I have to-day seen at least thirty feet of water in an immense disused chalk-pit, which a week or two ago was dry. All that water will, of course, filter away into the chalk by the time summer is here and water is scarce. This is the way all over the country. It amazes me that the gentlemen who sit in quarter sessions take no notice of it. Our new system of thorough drainage carries the water to the rivers with such rapidity that a flooded district may be dry in a few days.

I pass from water to Burgundy. The transition is not too abrupt; for in aguish, aqueous days few things are so cheering as a glass of

Burgundian wine. I have just been looking at a letter written by the great Erasmus in 1498, wherein he mentions his delight at first tasting Burgundy: 'O felicem vel hoc nomine Burgundiam, planeque dignam quæ mater hominum dicatur, posteaque tale lac habet in uberibus!' Suffering yet victorious Erasmus!— the real light of Protestantism, though he died a Catholic, the progenitor of modern thought, the most voluminous yet the most luminous of writers. No man has done so much literary work as Erasmus, yet no man is less known in this quasi-literary age. His fertility is without parallel. I do not believe there is a man living who has read all his works. He was the victorious champion of free-will against the narrow Fatalism with which Luther would have fettered the religious belief of Christendom, and for this alone deserves to be better remembered. Yet probably ninety-nine out of a hundred among our miscellaneous readers know nothing more of him than is told by Tom Hood's verses, written in 1835, at that 'vulgar Venice,' Rotterdam :

> 'And now across a market
>   My doubtful way I trace,
> Where stands a solemn statue,
>   The genius of the place;
> And to the great Erasmus
>   I offer my salaam,
> Who tells me you're in England,
>   And I'm at Rotterdam.'

No matter; if the man is almost forgotten, his work lives. His thoughts are uttered to-day by those to whom his name has no meaning.

Jan. 7.

A friend of mine the other day remarked that he did not see why there should not be a Government official in every parish for the faculties of law and medicine as well as divinity. Of course, we know that there is a parish doctor; but this did by no means fulfil my friend's idea. He thought there ought to be a kind of medical Rector, with power to look after the health of all parishioners, rich or poor, and to admonish them if they broke the stringent laws whose infraction always leads to disease. He also thought he should like a legal Rector, to whom everyone might resort for advice when quarrels arose, and who would have authority to settle at once vexatious litigations. Possibly, officials of this kind would be of more use than some who hold sinecures at the present day. A parish lawyer might do more good than a parish beadle or a parish constable. I was once elected parish constable myself, about ten years ago, but I took no notice of the election, and have not yet been fined for not serving. Choosing parish constables while you have a county police is like running an old-fashioned stage waggon in rivalry with the railway.

My Utopian friend, whom I may mention is Æsop Mactangent, F.R.H.S.—which he laughingly declares to mean Fellow of the Royal Hysterical Society—broached another idea that pleasant evening. I may remark that we had dined; that the woodcock had just been carried through the kitchen to have a feeling of the fire; that there was some sound port, which is nowaday a rarity; and that a lady whom the Utopian calls his Fairy was roasting chestnuts for us. She always boils them first, I may observe. Well, Mactangent, having given me his opinion about public doctors and lawyers, and burnt his palate with the hottest and flouriest of chestnuts, made another proposal.

'The Romans,' he said, 'had Censors. I would have them, on the same principle, in every parish of England. To quote, as well as I can from memory, an authority on this matter, ' they were to censure and punish evil and indecent manners, such as the law took no cognizance of, by degrading the senators and knights, and disfranchising the commonalty." Now, there cannot be the remotest doubt that some such authority is wanted among us in England. You cannot take a girl before a magistrate for looking as if she was ready to talk to the first young fellow she meets. Now if there were a parish Censor, with power to inquire whether that finely-dressed minx paid for her finery, whether she was justified in dressing herself up so radiantly, whether she did her work at home or left her mother to make the beds and peel the potatoes, and to order her what Fielding calls a little " stripping and whipping" if the answers were not satisfactory, how much good might be done!'

'How would you like the Censor to call in upon you?' I replied. 'I have known you to suffer from gout, which you consider hereditary: the Censor might differ from you, and stop your allowance of port wine. Then, to touch a delicate subject, there's your only daughter Helena' (he had named her after Troy's heroine) —'she is excessively beautiful, and dresses charmingly, but would not the Censor deem her comparatively useless? Would he not insist on her going to scrub kettles at South Kensington under Buckmaster? I am willing to have a Censor of morals if he looks well after the rich as well as the poor. Indeed, he ought to begin at the summit of society to be of any real use. Give him power to say to a Prince of the Blood Royal, "You have done wrong, and I degrade you," and then he may be serviceable. But a parish Censor in our times would be just like a school-board official, who worries the poor people to whom their children's services are necessary, but dares not enter a patrician drawing-room and find out whether the girls and boys of the establishment are properly educated.'

'Ah,' said Mactangent, 'it shouldn't be so if I were Prime Minister. I wish I were a Bismarck for England. I'd save the country from the inevitable ruin that's coming on it. Every boy should learn Greek, Latin, mathematics, and a trade, and at twenty-one should serve three years in the army. I wouldn't except the Prince of Wales. Every girl should learn reading and writing and arithmetic, cookery and needlework. Let them learn anything else they like, but *that* they should learn. What think you, Cæcilius?'

'I think that what you propose will happen when the Pope, to quote *Punch*, proclaims himself fallible, for a change—and not much before that time.'

* * * * *

Odd mottoes the rich people of the present day seem to get upon their plate and porcelain. They like Latin, and the longer the words the better. On the heavy silver of a millionaire the other day I encountered the wretchedest bit of Latin. It seems to me that in the present day the heavier the silver and the more the syllables of the Latin motto, the better it is thought in each case. However, leaving Latinity alone, certain is it that nothing should be heavy which you use for food. The weight of a spoon or fork seems nothing when you take it up, but using it for a considerable time necessarily tires you to a certain extent. Hence every utensil should be made as light as possible. Why should a glass be four times the weight of the wine it carries to your lips? To revert to the motto question: Might not the manufacture of mottoes for millionaires bring some scholar a bread-and-cheese income? I recommend punning mottoes—the Onslow 'Festina lente,' and the Vernon 'Ver non semper viret,' find parallel in Dean Swift's invention for a tobacconist, 'Quid rides.'

Mr. Auberon Herbert, who longs for that millennium when there is to be a piano in every cottage (at which period I certainly shall emigrate), seems to have taken up those unhappy New Forest Shakers, whose early extinction I predicted. When I wrote of them I had simply seen a laudatory description in the *John Bull*, and of course could not conceive that they were akin to the nasty American sect described by Mr. Hepworth Dixon. Something of that sort they seem to have been; a herd of illiterate, vulgar, excitable people, led by an elderly servant-woman. How Lord Carnarvon's brother can sympathise with such creatures I cannot understand. I knew Auberon Herbert before he became crotchety, and liked him thoroughly. Now I can only wonder what mad thing he will do next.

Talking of this maniacal affair, led by a servant-woman of low intellect, let me say a word or two on servants' literature. Servants *will* read, you know. In great houses I think there ought to be a well-chosen library for the servants, and they should be supplied with respectable newspapers. The cost of this arrangement is well repaid by results. As I said, they *will* read. If you do not give them wholesome mental food you will find they buy the *Police News,* all horror and pictures; or some wretched American nastiness, brought by tramps, full of vile stories and indecent illustrations. *Experto crede.* Such things I confiscate when they come in my way; but then I live in a cottage. If any reader of mine who lives in a castle or a mansion will entertain the idea of giving his servants a library of their own, I shall be well pleased. It ought to be done.

Jan. 12.

Chaucer has been familiarly called 'the well of English undefiled,' in forgetfulness or ignorance of the fact that he used French words as freely as English. In such a line as

'He was a verray parfit gentil knight,'

our great master of poetic narrative was almost wholly French. How could he be otherwise, seeing that he wrote the language of the Court, which was more French than English? He, in fact, was the first to form what is now called the King's or Queen's English, a phrase which, in the first instance, arose to describe the language in which Royal proclamations were made, as distinguished from the numerous local dialects which existed in England five centuries ago. Confirmation of this is found in the fact that such documents were written in what we still know as Court-hand.

A lady of my acquaintance who had to give out the books at a small parish library, in the absence of the regular official, was amused to find among them an old work entitled 'A Short Method with the Deists.' So well-thumbed was it, that clearly it was more popular (at least with the old women) than volumes of the *Leisure Hour* and the *Sunday at Home*. Suspecting that there was no borrower of books in that village who had the vaguest idea what Deists were, I inquired of one intelligent old lady of eighty who had read the book, and she defined them as ' people as wouldn't pay their Church-rates.' Now, a parish lending-library is a capital thing, but I think a book about Deists is not fit to be placed in it. Why should these poor creatures who struggle to be Christians be told that Deists exist? If Deists are to be described, why not Calvinists and Lutherans, Sabellians and Arians, Supralapsarians and Sublapsarians, Swedenborgians and Shakers? And I venture to think that the periodical works which are specially devoted to religious tales and essays are not quite food enough for the village mind. Good in their way, they should be supplemented by others.

Jan. 14.

Sir John Lubbock might well have placed on the title-page of his new work, 'On British Wild Flowers Considered in Relation to Insects,' the beautiful line from the 'Geörgics :'

'Admiranda tibi levium spectacula rerum :'

capitally rendered by Mr. Blackmore :

'The admirable drama of small things.'

Careful study of the way in which flowers are fertilised shows almost certainly that those which have the highest beauty of colour depend on the visits of insects whom that colour attracts. Whether the flower first fascinated the insect, or the insect developed the flower, is almost as hard a problem as whether the hen or the egg was first created—the probability being in favour of a creative development so well-balanced as to be almost simultaneous. Sir John Lubbock's little volume, written in the clearest style and accurately illustrated, will bring news to many even of those who have studied flowers or insects or both. Yet, as he says, 'our knowledge of the subject is in its infancy'—'few of those not specially devoted to zoölogy and botany have any idea how much remains to be ascertained with reference to even the commonest and most abundant species.' An example or two will suffice to show the curious interest of this study. There is a purple orchis, *Epipactis latifolia*, growing about two feet high in our English woods and shady places: it is fertilised exclusively by wasps, so that, 'if wasps were to become extinct in any district, so would the *Epipactis latifolia*.' The larkspur or *Delphinium*, of which a lovely variety, *D. formosum*, is common in our gardens, is fertilised only by the *Bombus hortorum*, a species of bee akin to the humble bee, but having a much longer proboscis. Anyone who has a bed of this rich blue flower may soon see its favourite visitor.

Sir John Lubbock remarks that he has been 'good-humouredly accused of attacking the Bee, because he has ventured to suggest that she does not possess all the high qualities which have been popularly and poetically ascribed to her.' Yet, though he does not believe in the 'moral and intellectual eminence' hitherto ascribed to bees, he maintains that to them and other insects 'flowers are indebted for their scent and colour; nay, for their very existence in its present form.' Had Virgil lived to see the results of modern science, he would hardly have written the noble lines in which he attributes a divine intelligence to bees.

※ ※ ※ ※ ※

Sir Robert Carden has excited just indignation in the breast of 'A Colonel' by telling a young fellow employed as a letter-sorter or carrier, who enlisted in the Guards, that it was a terrible mistake to make, that it would have broken his mother's heart, that in effect it was much better to sort or carry letters than to fight for England. Doubtless this was a foolish boy, and would have made a poor soldier, since he was in such a hurry to pay the 'smart-money' and be free again; but I hope our magistrates and aldermen are not going to preach old womanish doctrine of this kind. I hate war as much as most men; but the history of humanity too surely shows that without short sharp wars there can be no long calm intervals of peace. War is terrible enough, but it brings to the front the noblest attributes of mankind; and I protest against authoritative statements to the effect that a letter-carrier is better than a soldier. Sir Robert Carden has the fine old English title of *Alderman*, which once meant far more than it does now—'Ealdorman or Alderman, that is of course simply Elderman, used to be the highest title after King, just as in other countries you find rulers called by other names which at first simply meant *old men*, such as *Signore* or *Seigneur* (senior); so in

Latin *Senator*, and in Greek γέρων.' And if the Aldermen of England had not fought for freedom a thousand years ago, there would be no Aldermen of London to put letter-carrying above soldiering in these later days.

Jan. 23.

Admiral Sir George Westphal died on the 13th at Brighton, ninety years old. He was one of the noble relics of a great generation. He belonged to the time when, to quote Prince Bismarck, England fought one half of Europe and subsidised the other half. Be it always remembered that Prussia was our close friend in those old days, and that but for Prussia we could not have won Waterloo, and extinguished 'the meanest man of men,' Napoleon Bonaparte. Sir George Westphal was mate of Nelson's ship, the *Victory*, at Trafalgar; he was wounded in the fight, and Nelson's coat was used in the cockpit as a pillow for his head. When the great admiral, wounded to death, was carried down, his first exclamation was, 'What! poor fellow, are you here too?' The tenderness of truly brave

Thoughts in my Garden.

men is always noticeable. Nelson, who 'hated a Frenchman as he did the devil,' and who, Admiral Morris told me, always went into action in a rage that made him white as death, was under ordinary conditions as gentle as a girl. He had a touch of Sir Philip Sidney's temper.

The famous signal—

'England expects every man to do his duty'—

was, according to Sir George Westphal, actually given—a point about which doubts have been expressed. The great admiral proposed to signal—

'Nelson expects every man to do his duty.'

But several flags would have been needed to signal *Nelson* (though surely *one* flag ought to mean the admiral commanding), so the signal was changed to *England*, which required one flag only.

At the same famous battle, Sir George Westphal had a happy escape from death. 'The English fleet was bearing down upon

the French, the latter keeping up a brisk
fire, and, by order of Nelson, the British not
returning a single shot. Sir George and a
midshipman, eager spectators of the event,
were looking out of one of the portholes of
the *Victory*, watching the shot cutting up the
water, or rushing overhead. Mr. Westphal
had been enjoying the sight for some time,
when his companion, growing impatient, pulled
him back, saying, 'Come, it's my turn now,'
and looked out. That instant a shot came
and carried off his head. Thus one young
sailor was taken, and the other left; and Sir
George has remained among us till a week
ago, to remind us (we often need reminding)
of the great deeds of our fathers and grandfathers, the men who maintained English
freedom when the world was appalled by
military tyranny. They have left us a heritage
of greatness which should be imperishable.

* * * * *

I had the pleasure, the other day, of en-
tertaining a famous whist-player.* I never

---

* The well-known 'Cavendish.'

learnt so much about cards in so short a time. I am not certain that all this knowledge was not too much for me, as I woke next day with an awful headache, which made me curiously disinclined to do any work. Indeed, I dreamt all night of knaves dressed like fiends, with horns, hoofs, and tails of the most frightful colours and dimensions. He informed me that during the last ten years he has played twenty thousand rubbers at whist, and won about two thousand pounds. Is the game worth the candle? I was surprised to find he was quite ignorant of quadrille, and knew nothing of the Italian tarots.

Feb. 11.

The head-master of Christ's Hospital has recently written a letter to the *Times* suggesting that something should be done in honour of the centenary of Charles Lamb's birth. His chief idea seemed to be the foundation of 'English essay prizes.' I fear that no prize-giving can revive the English essay, specially as Charles Lamb wrote it. I open the 'Essays of Elia,' at one entitled

'The Old and the New Schoolmaster,' and find this delightful sentence: 'One of these professors, upon my complaining that these little sketches of mine were anything but methodical, and that I was unable to make them otherwise, kindly offered to instruct me in the method by which young gentlemen in *his* seminary were taught to compose English themes.' Now it is quite clear that no prize for an essay could produce an essayist, any more than a prize for a sonnet could produce a fine specimen of that perfect gem of verse, whose rules cannot be taught even to people who write books about it. If Christ's Hospital were to offer this prize, proposed by its head-master, is it at all likely it would be won by an essay on roast pig, or anything thereto similar? What is an essay? It is merely an attempt, an effort, an endeavour. Half, ay, more than half, such efforts are failures. Charles Lamb is our chief essayist, even as Shakespeare is our chief poet; but to offer a prize for an essay like one of Elia's would be like offering a prize for a play like one of Shakespeare's. There are things which cannot be twice produced. The essay is dead; for the present, at any rate. Lamb's successor is more difficult to find than any man I know, except Shakespeare's.

Professor Masson has recently published a volume of previously-issued articles, entitled 'The Three Devils.' His idea, in the chief essay of his treatise, seems to have been to criticise certain poetic conceptions of the Devil, the assumed Antagonist of God, under various aspects. Every man has his own idea of evil. It is an insoluble problem for all who dwell within the limitations of a strictly tangible existence. Is there such an entity? Professor Masson offers us three examples. After all, would it not be wiser to leave all theories about the creation of evil to rest on the wisdom and will of the Creator of good? Milton conceives Satan as a simple rebel, an angelic Oliver Cromwell, to whom he might have been Latin secretary. Luther's Devil was a mere superstition. Goethe's Mephistopheles is a degraded fiend, who is better fitted to the Haymarket and the Burlington Arcade than to the nobler avenues of life. Indeed, he is a fiend you would cut dead, as beneath contempt. Professor Masson's trilogies are seldom worth much. Once he wrote an article on 'Paper, Pens, and Ink.' Some cruel critic remarked that they might be useful—with ideas. Alas, how often we encounter paper, pen, and ink, and not the ghost of an idea!

Now, gentle reader, a final word, semi-apologetic. (By the way, it ought strictly to be hemi-apologetic, as the rough-breathing was only turned into a sibilant by the rude Latins.) I am going to be brief this week. Why? A lady came to play chess with me this afternoon. She is the best lady chess-player that ever opened with an Allgaier gambit. Yet we did not play chess. Not a bit of it. We went in for theological controversy. I am orthodox, but she is orthodoxer. We utterly outdid Capel and Liddon. We 'found no end, in wandering mazes lost.' We

Thoughts in my Garden.   77

got so far into the depths of Thomas Aquinas and Ignatius Loyola that it is all I can do to save the post.

'Five minutes to seven, sir,' says my perfectly useless boy whom the village *will* call a *page*. I wish he was page enough to make a book. My notes must go.

Feb. 18.

Long ago I wrote some verses, entitled 'My Thrush,' to a minstrel of the air who brought me divine music in the fairest days of a delicious year. He sang

> All through the sultry hours of June,
> From morning blithe to golden noon.*

---

* These verses are considered quite a gem of poetry, but, unfortunately, the writer could not keep his enemy the 'bucolic lout' out of them, and so they are spoilt by the third verse. They have been quoted in a previous work, but are perhaps worth reproducing in this.

> All through the sultry hours of June,
> From morning blithe to golden noon,
>   And till the star of evening climbs
> The grey-blue East, a world too soon,
>   There sings a Thrush amid the limes.

Thoughts in my Garden.

I think his progeny must have increased and multiplied, thanks to my regular fights against the bird-murdering louts who used to haunt my neighbourhood, but whom, by persistently calling for the aid of the police, I have thoroughly discomfited. There are scores of thrushes now singing in the wildest way : as I

God's poet, hid in foliage green,
Sings endless songs, himself unseen ;
   Right seldom come his silent times.
Linger ye summer hours serene !
   Sing on, dear Thrush, amid the limes !

Nor from these confines wander out,
Where with old gun bucolic lout
   Commits all day his murderous crimes ;
Though cherries ripe are sweet, no doubt,
   Sweeter thy song amid the limes.

May I not dream God sends thee there,
Thou mellow angel of the air,
   Even to rebuke my earthlier rhymes
With music's soul, all praise and prayer ?
   Is that thy lesson in the limes ?

Closer to God art thou than I :
His minstrel thou, whose brown wings fly
   Through silent æther's sunnier climes.
Ah, never may thy music die !
   Sing on, dear Thrush, amid the limes !

write there is a young bird (I know he is young, for he has not yet caught the true tune of the mature singer) full within view, high on a lime tree, putting me out of conceit with what I am writing. How true is the cry of the old balladist:

> ' 'Tis merry, 'tis merry, in gay greenwood,
> When mavis and merle are singing!'

How true, again, that Shakespeare-touch of Browning's:

> ' That's the wise thrush, he sings each song twice over,
> Lest you should think he never could recapture
> The first fine careless rapture!'

That thrush sang in May, according to the poet's lovely verse; but this year the birds began long before St. Valentine.

CHAPTER III.

SPRING, 1875.

O swallow, flying by windy ways,
    Over leagues of white sea-foam,
To the nest you left in the autumn days
    Under eaves of an English home—
Voyage right swiftly, wandering bird,
    A speck in the distant blue,
For the pulse of life in the leaves is stirred,
    And white doves coo.

Have you wintered away in the Cyclades,
    Or on marge of mysterious Nile?
No matter, so that the summer sees
    You back in our western isle.
But come, more swift than the sailing ship,
    For the skies are calm and clear,
And I long to see your brown wing dip
    In stream and mere.

Thoughts in my Garden.

Yes, I long for the magic of indolent hours,
  The glamour of amorous eyes,
When the breeze which fluttered 'mid fern and
    flowers
  In the noon's rich languor dies,
When bees grow drowsy in honey-bells,
  And the brown lark sleeps in his nest,
And a vernal vision of gladness swells
    One soft white breast.

Yes, I long to float on a haunted lake,
  And the weary past forget,
And the thirst of my restless heart to slake
  With the songs of Amoret.
So, hither, swallow, from Memphian fane,
  Or Greek isle set in the blue :
Fly fast to your English home again—
    Love comes with you.

March 4.

A QUESTION of precedence occurred at a country house the other day, which reminds me of the problem Mr. Disraeli set for students of etiquette in 'Lothair'—namely, 'Which takes precedence in a county, the Lord-Lieutenant or the High Sheriff?' This difficult matter has not, I think, been settled in the judicial pages of *Notes and Queries*. However, at a country house the other day, a Judge of Assize was entertained. The lady of the mansion offered her arm to the High

Sheriff. The Judge remarked that he followed, but under protest. He was courteous, and I hold he was right.

Questions of precedence may seem trivial to Radical philosophers; but they are important in complex society, as showing where a man stands in the world. There is an historic lesson in the fact that an Archbishop is above a Duke, and a Bishop above a Baron. The Premier's question, as between Lord-Lieutenant and High Sheriff, presents this difficulty—they are co-ordinate resident representatives of the Sovereign, the one military, the other civil. In a conquered country, a true *provincia*, the military authority would be supreme; but in our English counties there is this difficulty, that the Sheriff, or Shire Reeve, is far older than the Norman Lord-Lieutenant. Hence precedency becomes a question between Saxon and Norman. As to the Judge of Assize I am clear. He enters the county as representative of the Sovereign, to do what no local authority can do. He is at that time the first man in the county.

Thoughts in my Garden.

March 11.

Is the spring at last coming slowly up this way, as Coleridge hath it in the most dainty-mystical of all romances? The bitter east has left us for awhile: will it soon be possible to loiter on lawns and beneath lime-alleys, and listen to blackbird and thrush without fear of rheumatism and diphtheria? Let us hope to echo the charming words of Catullus:

'Jam ver egelidos refert tepores'—

by the way, the Romans evidently took a vernal holiday instead of our autumnal one. The poet proceeds:

' Ad claras Asiæ volemus urbes,
 Jam mens prætrepidans avet vagari,
 Jam læti studio pedes vigescunt.'

I certainly always feel more disposed for wandering in spring than in autumn. After a winter's torpidity and enforced confinement to one's own hearth comes the natural desire to be in some fresh place; and, in good faith, if I had not to loiter on paper to-day, I think I should take a twenty-mile walk. In autumn, after a calm summer, I like to see the melancholy beauty of decay steal gradually over the woodlands I love best.

*   *   *   *   *

Libraries are collected in many ways. The *nouveau riche*, who with Mr. Cobden prefers the *Times* to Thucydides, and of course the *Telegraph* to the *Times*, orders a book upholsterer to measure his shelves, and to send in so many yards of vellum-bound books, so many russia, so many of morocco. There is an old story of George Hudson, in his days of railway royalty, ordering a pair of superb globes for his library at Albert Gate, and sending them back in a rage because they did not match. He could find nothing on the terrestrial globe to match Sirius, nothing on the celestial to match England. Then there are the crotchety book-collectors. I once knew a man in the pleasant, but too tepid city of Bath, whose library was all of books on chess, and a grand collection it was. The oddest part of the business was that he could not play chess; had not, indeed, even learnt the moves.

Thoughts in my Garden.

Well, I see it stated, on the authority of a Mr. Higginson (the weight of whose authority is to me unknown), that 'the library of Count Leopold Ferri, sold at Padua in 1847, consisted solely of the works of female authors, and amounted to thirty thousand volumes.' I should scarcely have thought the literary work of ladies could have reached to such an extent twenty-eight years ago; though now, when the average of new novel publishing in England is five volumes a week, of which probably four are by women, the position is changed. Six hundred volumes per annum would give us another thirty thousand in half a century. I wonder did Count Ferri read these books. Or was he, like my friend at Bath, a man who collected from curiosity, caring little for what he collected? I think the chances are he was a misogynist.

March 16.

'A she-correspondent for me, always provided she doesn't cross,' said (I think) Isaac Disraeli. How heartily I agree with him! The fact is more manifest nowadays, when the men who can write good letters to their friends have seldom leisure to do it. I am fortunate in having several she-correspondents (don't scowl, O critic! I'm the 'marriedest of men,' as poor dear Bob Brough put it in one of his choicest rhymes), and they generally send me something pleasant. This morning, for example, a lady writes: 'What grievous sin has the nation committed that we are afflicted with this weather? If Gladstone were in office I could understand it, but with a Tory Government one expects better things.' There's a little Tory for you. Surely Disraeli is wise in supporting Forsyth's Bill, if the ladies are all going to vote for him. That they will seems clear. He is quite the ladies' man among Prime Ministers, if only as the author of 'Henrietta Temple,' the most sentimental of love-stories, yet fuller of real comedy than a play of Sheridan's. Often I take down my copy to look at some of the conversations; it is part of a set that I picked up by accident, - which belonged to the Premier's butler, who bore the appropriate name of Grapes. How charming is Count Mirabel—a reflex of the inimitable D'Orsay, to whom the book was dedicated! 'Fancy,' he says, 'a man ever being in low spirits! Life is too short for such *bêtises*. The most unfortunate wretch alive calculates unconsciously that it is better to live than to die. . . . . The sun shines on all; every man can go to sleep; if you cannot ride a fine horse, it is something to look upon one; if you have not a fine dinner, there is some amusement in a crust of bread and Gruyère.' And again, when Count Mirabel is asked whether he is not afraid of being bored, he replies: 'I do not understand what this being bored is. He who is bored appears to me a bore. To be bored supposes the inability of being amused; you must be a dull fellow.' Doubtless a fair sketch of Count D'Orsay's character. One thing is quite clear to any reader of 'Henrietta Temple'—Disraeli is the ladies' Premier. No Prime Minister of England ever wrote such a charming love-story—or any love-story at all, so far as I remember.

Here is another scrap from another she-correspondent, received this morning, suggestive in its way: 'The Vicar of W. has joined the Band of Hope Temperance Society. . . . . By-the-bye, the curious part of the business is that he invests the greater part of his money in a monster brewery! This is a fact.' What are the hopes of the Church when clerical gentlemen do this sort of thing? I have always held that a priest in holy orders ought to belong to no society whatever, save that supreme society in which he holds dignity and responsibility. If the Church of England cannot make men temperate, will the Good Templars or the Band of Hope be likely to do so? It is painful to think that the old-fashioned parsons are passing away, and that when the question of Disestablishment is forced to the front there will be such an amount of clerical silliness to urge in its favour. What has become of Praed's vicar?

> 'His sermon never said or showed
>   That earth is foul, that Heaven is gracious,
> Without refreshment on the road
>   From Jerome, or from Athanasius;

Thoughts in my Garden.

>   And sure a righteous zeal inspired
>   The hand and head that penned and planned them,
>   For all who understood admired,
>   And some who could not understand them.'

I fear that this grand old type is dying out too rapidly, and that an irreverent parody of 'Come into the Garden, Maud,' is in many parishes the motto of the young parsons:

>   Come unto confession, Maud,
>   And kneel at my priestly feet:
>   Come into my room with its saintly gloom,
>   And delight my self-conceit.

March 18.

The close time for wild birds began last Monday, the 15th of March. I hope all my readers who live in the country will take care that the bucolic louts do not shoot down the beautiful birds whom the law protects. I have for many years been pleading the cause of the 'angels of the air' in prose and verse; perchance, now that the Baroness Burdett-Coutts has taken up the question, it may become fashionable *not* to wear feathers in the dainty hats and bonnets with which ladies adorn themselves. Kingfishers' plumage looks pretty in a hat; but how would the lovely wearer like to see a kingfisher shot as he flies across the river, looking like a feathered fragment of rainbow? Would she not shed a tear or two for the glorious bird's lonely mate?

Mr. George Bentley, the publisher, writes to the *John Bull*, rebuking a contributor to that journal who, in an obituary notice of the late John Timbs, called him 'poor old Timbs.' There were points in the notice showing that the writer had no reverence or courtesy—but this single matter is sufficient. Mr. Timbs was an admirable editor and compiler, and did his work faithfully. To talk of 'poor old' So-and-so in a half-contemptuous fashion is not worthy of a gentlemanly writer. Does this fellow, who has not done half Timbs' work, look forward with serenity to being called 'poor old' Something-or-other in a notice of his (let us hope) early extinction?

※　　※　　※　　※　　※

The bicycles are coming to the front. The champion is to race a four-in-hand from London to Brighton, or *versa vice*. All very fine, gentlemen; but you will discover your mistake in time. You have to use muscles unnaturally. I know two men who have had to give up the bicycle simply because it was knocking them into iotas of imbecility. And what pleasure is there in racing through the country on high roads at ten miles an hour? Oh, the *walk* for me! A knapsack, a map of the shire, and a pocket compass, and away I go to do my forty miles a day, choosing by-ways and field-paths, and sleeping at wayside inns—though now and then some country gentleman has given me a dinner and a bed, and found that he entertained an angel unawares. For ἄγγελος meaneth a messenger; and many a message of poetry or politics have I brought to dwellers in villages.

* * * * *

I have just been cutting down some trees. As I write, I see the chips flying from a fir that long has taken all the strength out of the lawn at the point where it stood. The wielder of the axe, a namesake of mine by the way, though whether kinsman or not I cannot guess, would in my judgment beat Mr. Gladstone himself in disestablishing trees. He works with a will. Firs, I find, have no tap-roots, but run out lateral roots to a great extent, whence they ought never to be grown on lawns. My woodcutter seems to find it requisite to refresh himhimself very frequently at the adjacent hostelry, which bears the poetic name of 'The Seven Stars,' and is kept by a man just like the portrait of Daniel Lambert on Ludgate Hill (does it still exist?), all but the pleasant expression of countenance. I wonder does Mr. Gladstone take a 'peck' jar of old ale out with him when he goes to thin the Hawarden woodlands?

* * * * *

I don't know when Sir John Lubbock's Bill for the Preservation of Ancient Monuments comes on, but it has my best wishes. Most important is it that all our great relics, from Stonehenge downwards, should be carefully guarded. I, who have walked through most English shires, and searched for all possible records of the heroic and religious past, feel that I have a right to speak strongly on the topic. Indeed, I should rather like to be a

Curator of Ancient Monuments at a reasonable salary. It would be great fun in fine weather.

* * * * *

My tortoise, who has lived on nothing in the greenhouse all the winter, is now prowling about the lawn, and wildly dissipating on dandelion leaves. What a strange torpid existence creatures of this sort seem to lead! They are meant for a lesson to us, doubtless; and I realise the extremes of movement, when I see in the blue sky my carrier-pigeons whirling at about a mile a minute, and on the green turf my tortoise walking a foot in the same time. Well, according to the Homeric hymn, the tortoise suggested the idea of the lyre to Hermes, son of Maïa, swiftest-winged of gods; so extremes meet in many ways.

* * * * *

Moody and Sankey are still before the world. Can nothing be done to prevent illiterate persons from exciting a crowd of hysterical servant-girls and barmaids? How far is the career of these conquering heroes due to the neglect and division of the Church of England? Such a revival as these two men of the lower class try to carry through is mere superstitious inebriety; they are exhibitions, like the Davenport Brothers. Certain persons with handles to their names, whose insignificance I have not fathomed, attend upon the platform: but we know who Mr. Cowper-Temple is; the name he bears, and the name he has assumed, were once associated with common sense. If that association is for ever sundered why should he not go and dwell with the irrepressible Girling, and aid her to set up a new boy-girlery, *vice* Miss Wood, transferred elsewhere?

Seriously, these things injure the cause of sound religion in England—the good old, healthy, reasonable religion to which our forefathers clung. What would Bishop Latimer have thought of these American tramps. Now, I say that a county member who inherits a great name (too great an inheritance for him, perhaps) has no right to drag it through the dirt of pseudo-religious anarchy. For my part, I'd have these two Yankees left to themselves; but that might be considered too severe

Thoughts in my Garden. 95

treatment in these mild, amiable, 'humanitarian' times.

I observed that these two fellows, at the request of a servant-girl, prayed for 'a lady of rank, *but* careless of her soul.' That disjunctive conjunction is charming. It reminds one of the great chemist who was described as 'Father of Chemistry and uncle of the Earl of Cork;' also of Lady Jones, who 'painted in water colours'—and 'of such is the Kingdom of Heaven.' Why should a lady of *rank* care more for her soul than anybody else? I suspect that profane and illogical prayer was sent in by some Irish kitchenmaid, who had just been scolded by the cook for leaving the saucepan dirty.

March 24.

Although the long succession of easterly wind has kept back the spring flowers, the birds appear to be arriving early and breaking early into song. This year there will be no need to quote Plautus—

'Metuo ne lusciniolæ defuerit cantio;'

for last evening two young nightingales were singing against each other in my trees. The earliest date given by Gilbert White, of Selborne, for the nightingale is the 1st of April; the latest the 1st of May.

I heard what White aptly calls the willow-wren's 'shivering note' on the 20th of March. The earliest date he records is the 17th of April; the latest the 7th of May.

Sir John Lubbock, in his charming work on the relation between insects and wild flowers, says (page 53):

'*Anthophora pilipes* and *Bombus hortorum* are the only two North European insects which have a proboscis long enough to reach to the end of the spur of *Delphinium elatum*. A *pilipes*, however, is a spring insect, and has already disappeared before the *Delphinium* comes into flower, which seems to depend for its fertilisation entirely on *Bombus hortorum*.'

Yet yesterday a pair of insects that strongly resembled the male and female *bombus* were flitting over my hyacinths. I mention this as a matter of suggestion to lovers of out-door science. A skilled writer might treat as wisely the connexion of birds with insects as Sir John Lubbock has treated that of insects

Thoughts in my Garden. 97

with flowers. I am no 'ologist' of any kind, I regret to say, but merely one who loves in leisure moments to witness

'The admirable drama of small things.'

It may be worth notice that my garden is not quite an acre, close to the high road on one side and to a frequented byway on the other. Some people, probably, would scarce believe how much life in bird, and insect, and flower so small a space may include.

March 25.

Among the questions which sometimes occur to me there are some which perchance may be worth stating. For example, what should a man do who is a Duke with half-a-million a year? Such men there are in these opulent days, and I understand they are commonly managed by committees. This is a time of committees, with limited liability. But what an awful confession of weakness is made by the man who cannot manage his own affairs! Is aristocracy extinct? Are the social duties of the peers of England to be forgotten? I never go into Covent Garden without remembering an old doggerel epigram called 'The Contented Man's Wish':

> 'If I had one garden, one field, and one gate,
> I'd not envy the Duke of Bedford's estate;
> That is, I'd not envy his grace's estate,
> If I had Covent Garden, Smithfield, and Billingsgate.'

One might be contented with less; but I ask, why has not the ducal owner of Covent Garden wisdom enough to live in a princely way in that part of London of which he is lord, instead of being content with a commonplace house in Eaton Square? Is an estate in London of less consequence than an estate in the country? Might not the ancient noble style of life be renewed with advantage?

So of the Duke of Westminster. Half a city belongs to him, and he lives like an ordinary city man, at Prince's Gate—a haunt of wealthy city men. Why does he not build himself a palace worthy of his rank? I am glad to see him rebuilding his houses as the leases drop, though I cannot say much in favour of his architect: but architects are less numerous than dukes. Still, a Duke of Westminster, with such a grand estate in that famous city, ought to make his presence manifest. He ought to have a ducal palace, decorated with the noblest work of art; and to bring before the people the knowledge of what nobility means, he should employ great painters and sculptors. *Noblesse oblige*, say the French, and they are right.

* * * * *

Although the spring is late, the birds are early—a point which I am not ornithic enough to explain. The willow-wren is here. Gilbert White, our closest observer, whose favourite parish has given Lord Selborne his title, puts the appearance of this bird at from March 19th to April 13th. The skylarks have been singing to-day with a divine ecstasy that would have delighted Shelley. But the flowers are behind the birds:

> 'Daffodils
> That come before the swallow dares, and take
> The winds of March with beauty,'

show no sign of appearance within my borders; though

> ' Violets dim,
> But sweeter than the lids of Juno's eyes,
> Or Cytherea's breath,'

have been here for a long time. Which, I wonder, is the true queen of flowers? The wren, they say, is the king of birds, thanks to his having flown higher than the eagle by resting all the way on the eagle's shoulders. Human royalty often comes to the front by similar roguery. In these days of competitive examination, when everybody is expected to understand Sanscrit and the differential calculus, why should not the relative status of birds and flowers be determined? It might be done by a *plébiscite*, as the French call it. I think I should vote for the owl as king of birds and the white violet as queen of flowers:

> The owl that I see in an old forked tree,
>   With feather-lidded eyes,
> Is a king among birds, for he says no words.
> And he looks uncommon wise.
>
> The white violet amid green leaves set
>   Is queen of the flowers, I swear;
> For its blooms may rest on my lady's breast,
> And it finds Elysium there.

April 1.

Easter Monday invariably brings her Majesty's staghounds to Maidenhead Thicket: I was amused this year, as I have been for many a year, by the curious procession of people past my gate, which is about two miles from the place of meeting. I am not certain that if there were a parliament of horses, it would not repeal Sir John Lubbock's Act: for I saw plenty of parties of from six to eight drawn by a single horse, and in one case there certainly were twenty. The horsey captain in scarlet, who ogles all the neighbouring girls; the squire's groom, in irreproachable buckskins, on a fast mare, who declares his master keeps a hunter for *him* to ride; innumerable bicyclists, shortening their lives by abnormal and irrational exertion before they have begun to live: these were some of the Maidenhead pilgrims I beheld. I like to look at them. To me Easter Monday is no more a holiday than any other day; but then to me all days in which I have health and sunshine are holidays, for I love my work, and I wholly

agree in the great saying, *Laborare est orare.*
I add, *Laborare est vivere.* People are so
seldom content. A skilled artisan told me he
would like to be a clerk; a bank clerk, he
would like to be an actor or a scene-painter.
Now, to such folk I commend the homely
words of the Church Catechism: 'Do your
duty in that state of life unto which it has
pleased God to call you.' Heaven forfend I
should discourage a noble, healthy ambition;
but ambition will find an opportunity, while
the morbid craving for change always leads to
disaster.

*   *   *   *   *

I noted last week that I had heard the
nightingale and the willow-wren much earlier
than in any previous year, and I think that
birds and insects this year are curiously early,
though flowers are late. If Gilbert White, of
Selborne, were alive, he would make a capital
president for a society, to be spread over
England (and extended in time wherever
Englishmen dwell), which should take accurate
record of all ornithic, entomic, and botanic

facts. The connection between birds, insects, and flowers is so suggestive that really I think such a society should be started. I have not thought of a brief name for it. I have thought of a president: Sir John Lubbock is the very man, as we cannot resuscitate dear Gilbert White.

Such a society would have a wide field of investigation in the changes of the years. When we learn from Sir John Lubbock that there is an orchis which cannot live without the wasp to impregnate it, we have a faint clue to innumerable facts which can only be reduced to scientific system by wide observation and careful induction. Every year varies in its product of birds, insects, and flowers. I have heard it remarked that hornets are numerous about once in four years. This year is a good one for crocuses, a bad one for hyacinths. These subtle operations of nature are well worth investigation, for the more we know of the working of the world the nearer we are to the Maker of the world. So I wish somebody would inaugurate (I believe that's the penny-a-liner's word) the society I propose. The copyright is not reserved.

April 6.

I am the quietest man in the world, yet people will try to quarrel with me. The *Gardener's Magazine* is terribly angry with me because I happened to hear young nightingales singing on March 24th. It is an early date: had I not learnt the note of the nightingale in my boyhood, when I went to search for bee and butterfly orchises in Nightingale Valley, Clifton, I might be doubtful. But I live in a vicinage beloved by nightingales, and where they often keep me awake at night. It is suggested by my critic that perchance I heard 'two thrushes, or two woodlarks, or two robins, or two blackbirds.' If he were on my lawn for half-an-hour, he would know that no such mistake could well be made. Three robins talk to me as I pass under the trees, and I know their several notes. I have blackbirds and thrushes and missel-thrushes, and know their beautiful voices perfectly. No; it won't

do. Ornithology is not an exact science. I
have heard the same birds since.

The editor of the *Gardener's Magazine*, Mr.
Shirley Hibberd, is a gentleman for whose work
in the world I have high respect. His books
are on my shelves. But he ought not to
permit a contributor to imagine that there was
any epigram in ' ! ! ! ! ' No number of notes
of 'admiration' (*sic*) will make an epigram.
That I heard the nightingale a few days earlier
than Gilbert White is certain, and is worth
recording in connection with this curious
season. My critic is tremendously severe on
me because I say they were *young* nightingales,
and jumps to the conclusion that they were
this year's birds. If I called somebody a young
girl, would it mean she was a baby in long
clothes? By a young nightingale I mean a
last-year's bird, whose song is imperfect for
want of practice. All song-birds begin ten-
tatively, and improve as they grow older. The
young thrushes get finer song every day, as I
have reason to remark just now.

My critic says that the 'nightingale of the

newspapers sings *a month or two* in advance of the Philomela of poets and naturalists, and is audible only to those who cultivate the *belles lettres*,' etc., etc. I am amused to see poetry put on one side, and the *belles lettres* (an obsolete foreign term) on the other. I should have thought that the accomplished editor of the journal in question, who has *himself* ' cultivated the *belles lettres*,' would hardly have treated with absolute contempt the independent observation of one who, though no ornithologist, is philornithic, and who, perhaps, knows more about nightingales than most men. I have been brought into contact with several wonderful snarers of the *luscinia*, and when there's nothing else to write may possibly loiter among my ornithic reminiscences. And at this moment, if anybody wants a nightingale, I can tell him where one is to be found.

The gentlemen who abuse me in the newspapers are almost always kind enough to send me a copy of their paper, and for this I am much obliged. After more than a quarter-century of strenuous journalism, it would be strange if I had not trod on somebody's literary or political corns, since at all times I have spoken out my mind. Well, I get my critics and criticisms, and hope I profit by them, since it is never too late to mend, as Mr. Charles Reade has remarked—since also that in my belief the criticisms of the lowest creatures are worth calm consideration from the higher. If a man could get at the opinion of his horse or dog, or even his pig, as to his actions, it would be worth his while to think over it. In the same way, the general judgments of inferior people, even if hostile and splenetic, are worth weighing. I am much obliged to anyone who criticises me as savagely as he pleases in print, if only he will put a little intelligence into his criticism and teach me something. No one who attacks me need be afraid of an action at law, even should he declare that I murdered my great-grandmother. These things right themselves, and when I see London journalists raking up an old book of mine (which had its follies) I am simply amused.* Let them laugh

* The book alluded to was 'Sweet Anne Page,' one of the author's earliest novels.—F. C.

at me: why not? A lustrum and more has passed. 'I am no more ashamed of having been a Republican,' said Southey, 'than I am of having been a boy.' And I am no more ashamed of having written a certain book, which these people bring up against me at intervals, than Mr. Gladstone is of 'The Church Considered in its Relations with the State' (1840), or Mr. Disraeli of 'Vivian Grey' (1825). A man whose youth has no follies will in his maturity have no power. *Sic itur ad astra.* Sow your wild oats, and grow the wheat of wealth or the glorious grapes of genius.

April 8.

Dear Gilbert White is to be remembered by a restoration of Selborne Church, to which Magdalen College gives £250 and Lord Selborne £100. There is also to be a cross to his memory. I wonder what he would have best liked as a memorial. No such lover of nature have we had: he was the Shakespeare of birds. Were there a Chantrey to carve birds in white marble, in memory of him, it would be opportune. Is there no sculptor who could adorn that cross which is to be erected on the plaistor with a flying swallow in marble of Sicily? I don't see why all his observations of flowers and birds should not be recorded on the cross which is to do him honour.

*   *   *   *   *

The late Viscount Strangford's 'Angelo Pisani' is a wonderfully clever book, though it has no plot in the world. I assume everyone knows that he was the third of the Young England Triumvirate, Mr. Disraeli and Lord John Manners being the other two. He was, in fact, the original of Coningsby. He was a brilliant, irritable man, with no backbone to carry his rapid intellect fairly; and this novel of his really is worth reading, if for no other reason, as a mere psychologic study. The *Athenæum* seemed to think it ought not to have been allowed to appear, but in that opinion I do not agree. It is not a work of art, and if Lord Strangford had lived, he would doubtless have greatly changed it. But it is a work of genius; and the handiwork of genius, however inartistic, is always worth careful study.

April 15.

A correspondent objects to my remarks on Sir Richard Phillips, 'who did much good in his day by his intelligent and liberal publications.' Phillips published that vile book, Tom Paine's 'Rights of Man,' and was prosecuted for it, but whether imprisoned I forget. But whatever the good he did by his publications, I was dealing with him ethically as a publisher; and I say, that no man who, to use Peter Pindar's saying, drinks his wine out of the skulls of authors, deserves to be well spoken of. Phillips was an enterprising publisher, before his age in some things: he started the *Monthly Magazine* in 1796; he got men of genius and learning to write for him on starvation pay. What these men wrote benefited the world, doubtless; but meanwhile they were in misery, and this man was living in luxury, a sheriff of London and a knight, bless your heart! And I am to honour Phillips! Why, we shall have Curll, whom Swift so delightfully punished, set up as an idol next.

I am writing 'shop,' being myself a scribbler of long standing—one who, to use Thackeray's delightful Horatian lines, has had

> 'To joke, with sorrow aching in his head,
> And make your laughter when his own heart bled.'

Still, in these days, when letters are so widely cultivated, and when not only men and women, but actually little children, may be found writing books, the relation between author and publisher is of unusual interest. It is rather a curious relation, since it reverses the ordinary forms of business. Customarily, gentlemen want to buy; but an author is a gentleman who wants to sell. Now, nothing in the world is easier than buying, if you have money about you; and a gentleman comes in time to discover where he can get good fish, or wine, or game, or meat at a fair price, and to choose accordingly. I, a Londoner of long experience, can tell at a glance whether a shop of any kind is worth entering. Faith! though I belong to the inferior trouser-wearing sex, I can tell it of a shop where they sell bonnets or petticoats. But it took me far longer to find out where to sell my mental products. I know now. Experience has taught me who are the few London publishers who are gentlemen, and who can treat an author as a gentleman. There is a second class, who will not swindle you *much*. There is a third class, who will promise you a very small sum for your work, and never pay it if they can help it. I could 'name names,' as the Speaker of the House of Commons says, but my editor would cut them out. But once or twice I have been asked by strangers for a recommendation to publishers, and have invariably replied :

'Recommendations are useless. Go straight to So-and-so with your manuscript. He will have it carefully read, and will pay for it fairly if it has real value.'

This amount of guidance any author who has fought his way into literary smooth water would willingly give to a stranger; and if such advice were freely given, the publishing sharks of the Curll and Phillips class would have fewer victims.

As a Plymouth man, and a thorough lover of poetry, I am pleased to see a little volume of poems, 'the writings of nearly a hundred poets of varying merit connected with the two counties of Devon and Cornwall. Tamarland is poetic. A few of the men named and quoted in this volume were not known to me as natives of my own West Country. Of course I knew Edward Capern, the postman-poet, one of whose early books, with his autograph on the fly-leaf, is on my shelves. To be both postman and poet is very pleasant, but perchance the imaginative Devonian felt himself sometimes over-weighted by the possible contents of the missives he carried. Some of his wayside lyrics are very charming. Then there is Carrington—I am running through the alphabetic index—who caught the Solitary Spirit that seems to brood over Dartmoor, and caught the magic music of Dart river. Next, Coleridge—Devon's greatest poet—perhaps England's second. I don't know, judging by his quantitative limits of achievement, whether he was greater than Milton, Byron, Wordsworth, Shelley. I doubt if Shakespeare himself could have written such a poem as the 'Ancient Mariner.' Soon after comes Humphry Davy, the genius of chemists, who discovered potassium and the marvellous oxide of nitrogen, and who would, as Coleridge thought, have been a great poet had not chemistry been more fascinating than poetry. Whom else? Tom D'Urfey, the cavalier songster; John Gay, the fabulist; Gifford, editor of the *Quarterly;* Hawker, of the poetic parish of St. Morwenna; that wicked cleric, Herrick; Kingsley (the ode to the North-East Wind that has just killed him being quoted); Praed, our most polished producer of society verse; Sir Walter Raleigh, among the noblest of gentlemen; Nicholas Rowe, whilom Poet Laureate, and very clever when not writing in praise of Royalty; Wolcott (*alias* Peter Pindar), a thorough abuser of Royalty in the person of poor George III.; and Samuel J. Wesley, elder brother of the first Wesleyan. These are a few of the plums from a very poetic pudding, taken at random. I am glad my western kin can make so fine a show. The compiler is Mr. R. N. Worth, F.G.S. I don't know whether the 'G.' in those mystic letters means 'Geographic' or 'Geologic.'

The cuckoo was heard in Berkshire on the 12th April. This is five days later than Gilbert White's earliest date.

April 22.

It is curious to notice the magic of a night. One night's rain, and the trees are full of verdure. A red chestnut opposite my window, which yesterday had close compact buds only, is now stretching fans of green leaf towards the humid air. The expanding leaf of the red horse-chestnut—improperly so called, since it is the *Pavia rubra*, and not an *Aesculus*—seems like an aspiring hand, spread forth to catch the sunlight and the dew.

'Time,' said Hooker, 'is the measure of the motion of the spheres.' A better definition could not easily be framed. We divide our earth's year-travel and day-travel, and do our work accordingly. The sixty per cent. bill-discounter probably does not consider that three silver full moons will have shone on lovers loitering in leafy lanes, amid sweet chorus of the nightingales, before he can issue his inevitable writ. It is wise to think of the comparative ages of the creatures God has created. A gnat dies in a day, while a tortoise lives two or three centuries. Doubtless, *pace* Darwin, these differences were instituted for man's instruction. It is very sad, as I have lately proved, to lose by old age a dog that was yours in its youth. When a dog has been thirteen or fourteen years your friend, you have melancholy pleasure in tending his old age. 'Put him out of his misery,' says some well-meaning friend. I cannot see it. 'The whole duty of a dog,' said Christopher North, ' is to love man, and to keep his commandments.' It is a clear corollary that man should act with godlike tenderness towards his dogs.

Now, we compare our tenure of life with the dog's, and the comparison is a silent sermon. What if we compare our life with that of a tree ? Of course we may premise Ben Jonson's lovely lines :

> 'It is not growing like a tree
> In bulk doth make men better be ;
> Or, standing like an oak, three hundred year,
> To fall a log at last, dry, bald, and sear :
> A lily of a day
> Is fairer far in May ;
> Although it fall and die that night,
> It was the plant and flower of light.'

As I write I see many trees that I have planted on my lawn, and wonder who will enjoy their shade and bloom in days far off.* A distinguished naval officer recently had the courtesy to send me a paper on 'Indications of Spring,' read before the Royal Society, in 1789, by Robert Marsham, F.R.S., of Stratton, Norfolk. I find that he was a correspondent of Gilbert White, and a great planter of trees. 'An oak,' he writes in 1790, 'which I planted in 1720, is become now, at one foot from the

* Mortimer Collins had planted many of the trees in his garden, and tended them with loving care. Amongst his especial favourites were a Canadian oak, a red chestnut, a copper beech, and a medlar tree, all of which he planted when he first took possession of his cottage at Knowl Hill, in 1862.—F. C.

ground, twelve feet six inches in circumference, and at fourteen feet (the half of the timber length) is eight feet two inches. But I did not begin with beech till 1741, and then by seed ; so that my largest is now, at five feet from the ground, six feet three inches in girth, and with its head spreads a circle of twenty yards diameter.' Tityrus himself might have rejoiced in such a pœtulous beech grown in half a century. Mr. Marsham lived to ninety. To plant and care for trees is healthful work.

※ ※ ※ ※ ※

Friday, the 23rd of April, is Shakespeare's birthday. I think the birthday of England's greatest man ought to be a bank holiday, specially as it falls when ' comes in the sweet o' the year,' as the merry rogue Autolycus hath it. I am going to illustrate the event by a quiet little dinner, when libations shall be poured to a bust of the supreme poet, crowned with the *Laurus nobilis*, the poet's bay, that defies the lightning of Zeus. Could I afford it, I would give such a dinner as that devised by Colonel Sanderson at the Century,

New York, on April 23rd, 1860. The bill of fare, full of the most apposite quotations, is given in my friend Blanchard Jerrold's 'Epicure's Year-Book,' published in 1868 by Messrs. Bradbury and Evans. An example or two may amuse any reader who has not seen the original. The oysters of the first course, and their vinous accompaniment, were introduced thus:

> 'Sends
> This treasure of an oyster.'
> 'Set a deep glass of Rhenish wine.'

The roast lamb of the second course thus:

> 'Innocent
> As is the sucking lamb.'

While asparagus had the charming epigrammatic motto:

> 'Who comes so fast in silence of the night?'

Some blue-winged teal, in the third course, had the quotation:

> 'O dainty duck,
> With wings as sweet as meditation!'

Tutti Frutti ice-cream suggested a capital pun:

> 'Tut, tut, thou art all ice; thy kindness freezes.'

These are only a few points from one of the most epicurean bills of fare, and quite the most poetical I have seen. Of course the final motto was:

   'Some aqua-vitæ, ho!'

Colonel Sanderson, afterwards well-known in London as the able and courteous manager of the Langham, in this case struck out an original line, which those who love both literature and an artistic dinner might attempt to follow.

There occurred to my memory the other day a capital thing of Shirley Brooks's worth preservation. I had occasion to send him a letter from an editorial friend, who uses as crest a hand grasping a pen, with the apt motto, *Hinc orior*. 'An excellent device,' wrote Shirley in reply, 'but why does he spell *ink* with a *h*?' I call that as neat a classic pun as any of Porson's.

         April 27.

When I last week suggested that Shakespeare's birthday ought to be a holiday, I forgot to add that it is also the day devoted in the calendar to St. George of England: and I suppose England is the only country that does not annually honour its patron saint. The cry of 'St. George for merry England' was heard in many a famous fight, when the clothyard shaft of the English archer struck death through knightly coats of mail.

The Shakespearian dinner at the Century, which I mentioned last week, found a parallel in a dinner given at the Union Club, New York, to Edmund Yates, on the 21st February, 1873. Here, also, there was a Shakespearian quotation for every dish and wine; and some of them, as might be expected, are coincident. Two very good ones are:

COFFEE.

'The Duke of . . . Berry.'
Henry V., Act ii. Scene 4.

CIGARS.

' Whose smoke like incense doth perfume the sky.'
Titus Andronicus, Act ii. Scene 1.

On this occasion there was a list of guests, with a motto for each, and 'the guest of the evening' (as the penny-a-liners say) found himself confronted by a most apt quotation from 'Timon of Athens:'

> 'Even so, sir, as I say :—And for thy fiction,
> Why, thy novel swells with stuff so fine and smooth,
> That thou art even natural in thine art.'

Still, I think, if you give a man of letters a dinner, you ought to make all the mottoes quotations from his own works.

❊   ❊   ❊   ❊   ❊

I suppose we shall not get an Act this year that will do anything for the wild birds. Such very wild geese as Kenealy and Whalley are in the way of all useful legislation, and to shoot them (metaphorically, of course) with a double-barrelled gun would be a noble achievement. I caught a fellow yesterday trying to snare birds in my trees, and sent him off *pulice in aure*. He complained that I did not talk to him 'like a human being,' and suggested that of course I shot partridges and hunted foxes. However, I got rid of the fellow. One Sunday morning lately, a county magistrate, going across Maidenhead Thicket to church, noticed a couple of well-dressed men, who wore gold chains, lying on the ground. A little farther on he saw some cages set as traps for birds. Connecting these respectable persons with the cages, he ordered them to pack up their traps and be off. They insolently maintained their right to be there, so he walked down to the Coach and Horses to send a messenger for a policeman, and found they were putting up at that pleasant little inn, and had driven down in a handsome vehicle with a good horse in the shafts. They came down presently, and the worthy landlord soon frightened them into abject apology when he told them whom they had insulted. I suppose they will try another county next time. But how do bird-fanciers contrive to wear broadcloth and gold chains, and to drive fast-trotting mares in well-hung carts with red wheels?

April 29.

I learnt to read novels in my youth; for I was once at a school in a great naval port, where I was almost the only pupil not intended for the sea. My comrades were sons of admirals and captains, all panting to be midshipmen. It was a quaint establishment: the master, an indolent parson, used to make the upper form read a little Virgil in the morning and do a little Euclid in the afternoon, and even this he occasionally forgot. His second in command taught Navigation, and, I believe, nothing else. Now, as it was useless to waste that precious subject on a land-lubber like me, there were hours in the day when I had nothing to do. Luckily, there was a school library, full of old novels, and I read every one of them—sitting in the playground while the others were at work, a chartered libertine. It was an easy time. We had a dip in the sea twice a day all through the summer, and sometimes thrice. The master who taught Navigation was very sharp indeed, and understood the art of castigation also; but I, not being designed for the Royal Navy, did not suffer.

Now, from my boyish recollection, I opine that those old novels were better than the new. They seem to me (and one or two that I have since resuscitated confirm my theory)

Thoughts in my Garden.

to have been written by men who had seen the world, and who had met the characters they portrayed. Nowadays it is quite another thing. Female authors have come to the front, since the publishers find them cheaper; they mostly write for pin-money instead of a living. And what they write is seldom matter of experience, but is commonly a condensed day-dream of what they should like to happen. When a girl-novelist analyses all her feelings—strips herself naked, as it were—other girls rush to read and compare notes, and thence a fashion has arisen which most of the male novelists have thought it best to follow. They don't succeed very well, for an obvious reason: the girl in her teens who is the favourite heroine of the day is the most difficult creature in the world for a man to understand. She is in a mentally gelatinous stage, with nothing about her firmly formed. Wise writers would leave her in the nursery somewhat longer.

These reflections are suggested by Mr. R. D. Blackmore's 'Alice Lorraine,' in which there are a couple of heroines, both rather younger than I care about, but both healthy and girl-like. Mr. Blackmore is the most idyllic of novelists: his sketches of Covent Garden Market, A.D. 1811, in the early morning—of the delightful cherry orchards and strawberry gardens of Kent—are poems in all save metre. The book is one to read.

*　　*　　*　　*　　*

So long have I been accustomed to admire Shakespeare's cool way (in 'The Winter's Tale') of making Bohemia a maritime country, that I was rather disgusted to find in Hamner's edition (Clarendon Press, 1770) the suggestion that Shakespeare wrote 'Bithynia,' and that 'the ignorance and negligence of the first transcribers or printers' caused the blunder. Well, printers have been very guilty of many errata; but I think in this case it was the easy carelessness of the great poet, to whom geography, like chronology, was a matter of no moment. In this age of rigorous exactitude, the *Saturday* would doubtless ridicule him much; but I cling to Bohemia.

Ought all modern Bohemians to be renamed Bithynians?

May 4.

Whether there is any change in the seasons I know not: but certes, April is more like March than it used to be, and May more like April. May came in with what used to be called April showers; and I think we had better amend the old distich, and say that:

> 'April winds and May showers
> Bring in June flowers.'

By the way, the ladies will perhaps like to know that there is no cosmetic like a shower of rain. If you want to get a charming complexion, go out and get washed by the rain or the dew. What is the most exquisite reason? Chemistry answers the question: water falling slowly through the atmosphere absorbs oxygen, and oxygen is the great life-giving principle. Dew is better than rain, since it falls more slowly, and therefore absorbs more oxygen in its passage. An easy experiment will afford collateral proof of this: oxygen and hydrogen form water, and oxygen is just sixteen times as heavy as hydrogen; oxygenised water must, consequently, be heavier than ordinary water. Take a glass of spring water, and shake into it some dewdrops from the boughs—you will see them sink to the bottom of the glass. I wonder the perfumers do not prepare an oxygenised water for the complexion, which might be fragrant with lilac in May, and lilies in June, and roses in July, and so forth; but perfumers, for the most part, have neither chemistry nor poetry. However, it is better for beauty to find its own cosmetic in the dew that lies upon the leaves in happy summer morns.

Now this suggests one of the favourite follies of the time—a double acrostic. It shall be a very short one.

'Tears from the flushing eyelids of the Morn:
Delicious deed—for this was Beauty born.'

I.

'Of cleric habit, you shall see him perch
And preach his sermon—but outside the church.

II.

She brought us trouble in the ages past:
Whate'er our trouble, she brings rest at last.

III.

Arrows are this, and seraphim, and birds,
But above all (see Homer *passim*) words.

Now I have not made that up, as do most of our acrosticists, from geographical and classical dictionaries, selecting the most difficult and break-jaw names. The double acrostic was a pretty notion, whoever invented it; but it is a sheer piece of stupidity when based on barbarisms. What I have given is curiously easy; but difficult ones can be composed without the aid of dictionaries—without introducing words that are no more words than a backgammon-board is a book.

The metastich is rather a pretty poetic puzzle. Take a line of some classic poet, and imbed it in a stanza, one word in each line. The following, for example, contains a blank verse line from Ben Jonson:

> Comes the Spring, when men who are wise
> Welcome the May, and girls demurely
> Out in the woods will flirt securely—
> Where is the sin of such light love-play?
> O but the prying prudes have eyes!
> Safely to flirt is impossible, surely;
> Never one knows what the world will say.

May 6.

Dr. Wynter, who has among his essays one on precious stones, is asked why he does not explain the difference between a red diamond and a ruby, or a blue diamond and a sapphire. I should have imagined this piece of information hardly worth giving. The diamond is pure carbon, whatever its colour may be: the ruby and sapphire are rhomboidal crystals of corundum, of which the sesquioxide of aluminium is the chief base. When chemistry reaches perfection, probably we may get diamonds from charcoal, and sapphires and rubies from alum.

I am always amused by the droves of cattle coming from Reading fairs, as they pass my gate. There was a fair on the 1st of May, and cattle were passing in an interminable procession all the afternoon. Up to this they have traversed a monotonous road; but here there are shadowy trees on one side and a green hill common with great stretches of yellow furze on the other. That common is too much for steers and heifers. Away they canter, heads down and tails in air, into the green and golden paradise. The drovers have a *mauvais quart d'heure*. They shout frantically, using the strong but limited language of execration which the British peasant seems to learn in his cradle. Often I wonder whether the School Board will be able to teach the next generation of working men a more elegant style of invective. With every herd this stampede occurs; and, watching the proceedings, I hold that a drover ought to have rather more patience than Job—or than the House of Commons when Kenealy and Biggar and Sullivan come to the front.

May 13.

I was surprised to notice in the University intelligence of the *Times* that the prize for a certain Cambridge essay was not adjudged last year, though the theme was so fascinating as the limits of man's rights over animals, and his duties to them. I quote from memory, as my *Times* of that special day has vanished. But really one would have thought Cambridge men, of whom a large majority must be familiar with horses and dogs, and not these only, but oxen and sheep, and pheasants and partridges, would have been glad to write on a subject so interesting and important. I quite regret I am not an undergraduate. I should have put as a motto to my essay Chaucer's description of the conduct of the Prioress to the dogs :

'. . . . She fed
With roasted flesh and milk and wastel-bread,
But sore she wept if one of them were dead.'

I should have written down the *battue*, but used all my logic in favour of fox-hunting. 'The men like it, the horses like it, the dogs like it, and we can't be sure that the fox doesn't like it.' At any rate, if he does not, brown Reynard is in a hopeless minority—just the position of the gallant O'Gorman. Really I am sorry the 'young barbarians' of Cambridge found that essay too much for them. Surely some dog-loving undergraduate might have shut himself up with his favourite bull-terrier, and got a few ideas out of him.

* * * * *

I have received a volume of poetry, entitled 'Wind-Tossed Leaves,' by Charles Curle—a friend I have not seen for many a year. These poets—they will go on: I had hoped he had given up bad habits long since, and become a steady stolid member of society, and a director of several companies. I find on page 83 some sapphics *ad Cæcilium*, written fourteen years ago.* Thus commence they:

> 'Many pleasant hours we have passed together,
> In the silver lamplight, heedless of the weather,
> When from arduous duty loosened was the tether,
> Tendit Apollo.'

After some pleasing remarks on my per-

---

* These papers were signed 'Cæcilius.' The lines descriptive of Mortimer Collins's appearance were:

> 'Handsome in appearance, firm, but ferocious,
> Good in classic scholarship, ripe grown, not precocious;
> Equally at home with Rabelais or Grotius,
> Et decus omne.'—F. C.

sonal appearance, which I modestly suppress—
since fourteen years *do* make a difference—he
proceedeth :

> ' Charming verse you give us in magazine or paper,
> Never indicating smell of midnight taper,
> Elegantly light is thy Muse's choric caper :
>   Hinc tibi plausus.'

I am impelled to say, in due response, to my
flattering friend :

> Now, do you think, O Carole Cincinne !
> That I, who earn my customary guinea,
> Am to be flattered, like a youthful ninny,
>   By your soft sapphics !
>
> Wheel of Ixion, rolling stone eternal,
> Pushed up by Sisyphus, toil for many a journal,
> Keeping me back from poesy's bright kernel—
>   These are my traffics.
>
> Well, we grow joyous at the cool regatta,
> Drank—was it Heidseck ?—shouted our *Thalatta !*
> Heard rippling Tamar murmur its cantata,
>   Mocking our laughter.
>
> And 'tis true pleasure, O Cincinne care !
> Far though we are from the region of Vagary,
> That we are able to conjugate *Amare*
>   Many years after.

CHAPTER IV.

SUMMER, 1875.

Oh, for a picnic, here's a place,
    When the hot noon of summer kindles !
Down by express to Taplow race ;
    Refresh yourself where once was Skindle's ;
Or row from Maidenhead, if you will,
    Along the river's loveliest reaches ;
Then take the road, and drink your fill
    Of coolness 'neath the giant Beeches.

Quoth Pet to me—she's mistress now,
    I mean to be her lord and master—
'Just corrugate your manly brow,
    And prove yourself a poetaster.'
Luttrel was told to do the same ;
    A lesson his example teaches ;
To an untimely end he came,
    Wanting another rhyme for 'beeches.'

'Pet,' I replied, 'some lobster first—
　This fellow's the true Norway crimson;
A goblet then to quench your thirst—
　See the bright wine the bubble swims on.
Now, would you like a slice of pine,
　Or one of those voluptuous peaches
Touch'd with a colour half divine,
　Like sunset seen through Burnham Beeches?'

Ah, what a wicked witch is Pet!
　Although so carefully I fed her,
And then, as far as we could get
　From her mamma, I briskly led her;
Although we criticise the trees,
　And wonder what the tale of each is,
Yet she returns to—'Charlie, please,
　Do write some verse on Burnham Beeches.

'Do quiz dear Amy, getting spoons
　Upon that gawky little cornet;
And Mary, with big eyes like moons,
　Fainting because she saw a hornet;
And grim old Sophonisba Snooks,
　Who tries to flirt, but only preaches
Sermons on woman's rights, and looks
　A fungus upon Burnham Beeches.'

'Pet,' I replied, 'your rosy lips
　Were never meant for words satiric,
From graceful head to finger-tips
　Your every look's a living lyric:
I'll punish you for naughtiness.'
　'O don't, dear Charlie!' she beseeches;
Her penalty you'll have to guess:
　Secrets they keep, those grave old Beeches.

A strange magnificence of gloom
  Falls o'er the trees with falling twilight,
While hayfield's scent and lime perfume
  Delight us driving through the shy light.
Lo, as a mighty beech we pass,
  Close at our ears a brown owl screeches,
And wicked Pet exclaims, ' Alas,
  That's the true bard of Burnham Beeches!'

June 3.

SUMMER at last, apparently; but the wind lingereth in the east. There are people who don't seem the least to care from what quarter the wind blows, and I sometimes am tempted to wish I was one of them; but I change my mind when the sweet south arrives, for then I know that I have enjoyment which my pachydermatous fellow-mortals never can realise. Power of enjoyment and of suffering are in direct proportion. Talleyrand's theory, that all you want to be happy is a hard heart and a strong stomach, is quite true for certain natures; they are as happy *as they can be*— just like a pig in a sty, or the tortoise which I now see browsing on my lawn, and which simply sleeps through the winter in the greenhouse. But in contrast to that tortoise (from whose kinsman only Hermes could get music) there is a thrush on the very summit of a lime tree, trying to deafen me in his delight at the glory of June. He is positively shouting his joy. Ha! and now a blackbird has begun to mock him with a mellower note, as if Rossini echoed Verdi. I dare say, in sharp winter, when the pig was warm in his sty, and the tortoise snug by the greenhouse flue, those two choristers of summer were glad to pick up crumbs at my windows, and pined for their natural dinner of snails and worms. Yet, dear reader, which would you rather be—pig or tortoise, mavis or merle?

* * * * *

When I was a boy I could not get anybody to explain why equidifferent series were called arithmetical, and equirational geometrical. The elementary terms that have come to us from the clear-thinking Greeks are sensible enough. Cube is a die, and cylinder a roller, and sphere a child's ball, and pyramid a flame of fire, and cone a fir-fruit. All these mark the early growth of geometry from the first forms of things. They are natural and simple. Then it is to be remarked that Athens had no algebra and little arithmetic; theirs was the mathesis of form, and hence the curious beauty of their architecture, produced by strong sense and careful study of proportion.

It seems to me that there is room for a new art—the Art of Systematic Nomenclature. All sciences ultimately osculate, and it would be a wise thing to get their technical phrases somewhat in accord. Much would be done toward a science of sciences if we could agree on a vocabulary. As matters are, scientific language is simply barbarous. *It should never be forgotten that what we call science is merely the study of the world; that its special departments are simply the result of human imperfection, since a finite creature can only see one aspect of a thing at once; that the remote stars and the familiar flowers are controlled by the same Divine law; that separation of sciences is due to human infirmity.* Hence it seems to me that if a few of our foremost men in every department would concur to decide on a system of scientific nomenclature, it would greatly tend to the logical development of scientific discovery.*

* * * * *

Observers of nature cannot fail to perceive the infinite variety in the form of trees and plants, the movement and music of birds—supplying to the un-Darwinised mind clear proof that there is an infinite intellectual power controlling this Cosmos. I believe Mr. Henslow's theories on Phyllotaxis—the law which forms leaves and flowers—are very suggestive; but they have only been read, so far as I know, before a learned society. Their publication would be a stimulus to those who see the importance of investigating the law of order in nature. I believe it will in time be found that every growth of foliage, every flight

---

* It is probable that M. C.'s researches in science were not very deep. It is happily certain that they were not deep enough for him to lose his reverence for the Almighty. He was like Faraday, who, the more he discovered the more he reverenced. A widely different result from that attained and inculcated by the scientists of the present day. By the advanced thinkers of our age M. C. would be classed amongst those old fogeys who believe in the existence of an Almighty Being.—E. Y.

of bird in the air, has its mathematical equation. Michelet calls the swallow *l'oiseau de retour :* not only does it return on its own line of flight as it circles through English air, but it returns hither from unknown regions of Asia and Africa to the very same nest of the year before. Hard to find the curve of a bird's flight! I fancy the swallow swings in an ellipse, like this planet Earth itself. Certes, no two birds fly alike; no two trees grow alike. Men are the most imitative of animals (monkeys not excepted) save only women. City men, betting-men, M.P.'s, popular preachers, artists, may all be known by 'the cut of their jib.' Men move in cliques; you won't see a City man with long hair over his shoulders, or a rising artist carrying a small silk umbrella. But women don't thus separate; they all want to be of the same set. If you go into a country church you will see the squire's cook wearing a hideous caricature of her mistress's last new bonnet from Bond Street. The present tight-fitting dresses, capitally drawn by Du Maurier in last week's

Punch, fit a woman of fine figure delightfully; but Miss Spindleshanks and Miss Bonyhips think they fit them too—and oh, the sad result! Dear young women, we can't all be handsome: but we can all be good, and abjure vanity and vexation of spirit. Thus dogmatises your Loiterer* when he sees some of you dress like Artemis, the queen of the mountains, at the bidding of your dressmaker, who knows very well that the wider your petticoats the better.

Still, we have the Artemis type among us: and I like a fashion that suits supreme beauty. An excellent parallel might be drawn between Fashion and Politics, if only one had time—and skill. Both want a leader. The leader of Fashion must be royal and pretty: the leader of Politics must be wise and witty. Both must think nothing about their followers, but amuse themselves with their own caprices. The perfect leader of Fashion should be a lady the colour of whose eyes and hair my readers are permitted to select, but whose figure must be faultless, and her utterance both music and

* Some of these papers were entitled "The Loiterer."

Thoughts in my Garden.

wit. The perfect leader of Politics may be as ugly as he likes, as eccentric as he likes, as inconsistent as he likes—aye, even as wicked as he likes; but he must have the genius that makes him hot as fire in attack, and cool as ice in defence: afraid neither of the leader of the opposition nor of the leading bully of Europe.

* * * * *

If Captain Boyton has succeeded in nothing else, he has made a good many 'gentlemen of the press' very wretched. Fancy twenty-seven hours in the Channel with a ground swell! Your Loiterer was not there; no, he loves the sea, not in a sickly-smelling Channel steamer, but on board a saucy cutter yacht, that can race at will and loiter at will. I cannot see that the gallant captain has proved much, or given us any definite help in the matter of shipwreck. The man who can use Boyton's apparatus with Boyton's pluck will scarcely need that apparatus in an emergency. He will cling to a spar and swim ashore somehow. Even if it were proved that it would be of use in case of shipwreck, it must be remembered that there are no kind creatures in the desolate seas to supply the green tea and beef sandwiches and cigars which seem requisite at intervals. Captain Boyton's invention will be admirable when mermaids turn barmaids. But, perhaps, if the mermaids *would* turn barmaids, we could do without the invention.

Still, the captain was a sensation, and just now sensations are popular. Frivolous people without definite occupation require them. Captain Boyton has crossed the Channel for a crotchet of his own, and declares that no amount of money should induce him to do it again. After this, seafaring folk will be shy of expending money in the captain's invention, unless they find it more easy to manage without the aid of green tea and sandwiches. But what is to come next? Boyton will soon be forgotten, and the Gadabout family will need something new. Will no chemist light London at night with a magnesium sun, suspended just above the Nelson Monument? How all the world and his wife would crowd from the

country to see that exhibition! Could not
Maskelyne and Cooke's 'Psycho' notion be
enlarged, and a theatre opened in which all
the actors are machines? Their elocution
could not be worse than that of some actors in
flesh and blood we might mention, and of
course 'gag' would be impossible. Will nobody invent wings, and teach the art of flying?
As I write I see swallows floating easily in the
air above me; and it certainly seems delightful to imagine such swift progress through the
calm air. I see the lark soar; the hawk hover
and dart; the swifts shoot past like a flight of
arrows screaming through ether; the pigeons
tumble as they fly; the owls sweep low in the
twilight, silent in their search for prey. Yes,
it would be rather nice to have wings. Yet,
consider what queer birds a good many of us
would make. I have several most estimable
friends who would not look at all handsome
perched, bird-fashion, on the gable of my
cottage. No; on due consideration, I will
decline wings at present.

Talking of birds, there has been in the *Times* a correspondence about rooks, and a learned pundit of the Temple, quoting Acts of Parliament passed in the reigns of Henry VIII. and Queen Elizabeth, maintains that anybody can shoot rooks in anybody else's trees. Can this be true? Would not there be a trespass if a man fired into a rookery? These old Acts seem to have enforced the destruction of rooks, crows, and choughs, because they were ignorantly supposed to destroy the grain crops; but as such notions are now obsolete, so ought the Acts to be. There is scarcely a fine country house in England without its musical familiar rookery; the cawing of the birds awakes one in the fresh summer morn, as they travel far afield; their evening utterance comes just in time to say that dinner will soon be ready. If rooks are not protected, they ought to be—and that at once. They are unmentioned in the schedule of the Wild Birds Protection Act, 35 and 36 Victoria, cap. 78. But then that Act was most unskilfully and absurdly drawn, and the birds named in the schedule seem to have been classed together by mere chance.

June 8.

Now this is the very time for loitering. Not with pen on paper, though, but under shady trees which hang over river margins or cool long slopes of virgin turf. However, my pen, and not I, must loiter to-day; and it is possible that anyone who saw me at work under full-leaved limes, with a red chestnut burning lamp-like flowers close by, and with a thousand birds talking and twittering (it is too hot for them to sing), would probably say I have no need to grumble. Doubtless the people at Ascot—which lies eleven miles from my gate—are much hotter and unhappier than I. They are poisoning themselves with petroleum champagne; while I, being, as is well known, a disciple of Sir Wilfrid Lawson, have of course a flask of toast-and-water cooling on the grass at my feet. The beauties of that beverage are not understood by the uneducated people who drink cheap wine in these days.

I see in Longman's last number of 'Notes

on Books' an account of a recently-published work by Mr. Girdlestone, rector of Kingswinford. The book itself (or rather pamphlet) has not reached me: but the idea is a good one, and I hope he has worked it out as well as it deserves. Its subject is 'Number'; and it strives to show that the understanding of Number shows alike a link between Man and his creator, a chasm between Man and the inferior creatures. This is clear enough to a disciple of Plato, but not to a disciple of Darwin. The most intelligent dog you ever had could by no means understand that the velocity of a falling body varies as the square of the time; that the planets in revolving round the sun describe equal areas in equal times; that when carbon and oxygen combine with each other it must be in similar proportions to their separate combination with hydrogen. Now, if King Atom makes all these delicate mathematical arrangements, he deserves Darwin's deification; but men, who look upwards by a glorious instinct, have a belief that it is some One far greater than

this infinitesimal Lord of Liliput. To carry
Paley's illustration a trifle farther, why in the
world, when sage atoms were combining to
form men and women, did they not also form
houses for them, and dresses, and watches, and
everything else conceivable for the need of
humanity? Mr. Girdlestone's argument urges:
'That the Mind which ordered all things, as
man finds them now existing, must have used
Number in every department of the Universe:
that the human mind has the faculty of understanding the relations of Number which thus
permeate all things, has also actually discovered and demonstrated them, and is, more-
over, able to use Number for very many purposes of its own; and that no other creatures,
as far as we know, can either use or apprehend
Number at all. Hence it follows, according
to the logic of probability, that the human
race is not the progeny of apes and ascidians,
but rather is, as the heathen of old concluded,
"God's offspring."' There is nothing new in
this, but if popularly stated it may serve to
show thoughtless people how wild current

theories of pseudo-philosophy have grown. Still, if monkeys could solve an equation, or light a fire, or make a tool, I should gravely doubt if I were a monkey's distant relation—cousin many times removed. Aware that an eminent mathematician of these later days believed in Spiritualism, I should not be surprised if you could teach the binomial theorem to a chimpanzee. There are men, even in Parliament, of whom the anthropoid apes might well be ashamed: but this does not show identity of origin. I suppose Kenealy or Biggar would be found to have some vague notion of the meaning of *time* or *space*—ideas which animals seem unable to comprehend in the slightest degree. Whether the lower animals have language or not is a moot question: but it matters little in connexion with this particular line of argument, since the lower classes of men are always the most talkative.

June 10.

I recommended a young lady of my acquaintance to read Coleridge's famous work on

'Church and State,' and she borrowed it from her parson, who remarked in sending it that it was deep but not very clear, and that she would not agree with many parts of it. Charming criticism! on one of the clearest yet wisest works ever written on this crucial subject. Do the clergy of the present day know anything about Coleridge? Perchance one might almost ask the same question as to St. Paul. So occupied are many of them with mere questions of ceremony that they altogether ignore theology. And what does true theology—the science of God—involve? Hear Coleridge: 'The Clerisy of the nation, or National Church, in its primary acceptation and original intention, comprehended the learned of all denominations, the sages and professors of the law and jurisprudence, of medicine and physiology, of music, of military and civil architecture, of the physical sciences, with the mathematical as the common organ of the preceding; in short, all the so-called liberal arts and sciences, the possession and application of which constitute the civilisation of a country, as well as the theological. The last was, indeed, placed at the head of all; and of good right did it gain the precedence. But why? Because under the name of theology or divinity were contained the interpretation of languages, the conservation and tradition of past events, the momentous epochs and revolutions of the race and nation, the continuation of the records, logic, ethics, and the determination of ethical science, in application to the rights and duties of men in all their various relations, social and civil; and lastly, the ground-knowledge, the *prima scientia* as it was named—philosophy, or the doctrine and discipline of ideas.' Now I diffidently venture to ask whether, in our modern conflict of creeds and ceremonies, the Clerisy are not beginning to lose sight of this wide field of duty? 'Altar or Table?—Alb or Cope?' and other fruitless alternatives, may seem important to those who think more of priestly dignity than of priestly duty. But duty confers dignity, and any man, as a mere labourer, may attain true dignity by doing his duty thoroughly, while an emperor may lose all claim to dignity by not doing his duty. Commonplaces these, you will say, friendly reader; but we can't do without the eternal enforcement of commonplaces. Looking through Coleridge's definition of a theologian, you find in him also the linguist, the historian, the logician, the moralist, the politician, the philosopher. That Coleridge was right is irrefragable; for theology means the science of God, and the science of God is the science of all things. Indeed, one might call theology the Proteus of sciences, since it changes its form perpetually. When a chemist discovers a new law or a new element—when a mathematician pushes forward the power of analysis, or finds a new planet in the supreme depths of blue—he is simply furnishing corollaries to astronomy—he is illustrating the science of God.

Hence, could we but sketch, with the pen of true genius, the model rector of an English parish, what a grand picture he would be on the canvas. Vandyke should paint him. The man who, with a clear view of the high central truth, has a deep sympathy with humanity in its worst troubles; who turns undazzled from the Great White Throne and carries its light into wretched hovels and into the minds of wretched men; who strives to interpret the thought of God by the work of what we call nature; who deems no science useless, no creature soulless—that is the true parson. He, the *persona ecclesiæ* (*vide* Blackstone), through whom sounds the Voice of the Church, should exhaust the knowledge of the world as a mere contribution to the infinite science of Theology. When we have such a clerisy as that, we need fear no disestablishment.

June 17.

Fair reader, do you wear fresh flowers in your hair every evening at dinner? I hope so. It is a charming custom. They are lovely to look at, delicious to smell. Ladies are (mercifully) made as a rule shorter than the less worthy sex; and when you take a pretty girl in to dinner, the moss-roses and honeysuckle in her hair heighten her fascination. The scent blends with that of the pine-apple at dessert and of the fragrant Mocha in the withdrawing-room in an exquisitely magical way.

> A whiff of eglatere from ladies' tresses
> A most magnetic mystery possesses :
> Twined in soft hair the happy floweret tries
> To imitate their beauty, fails, and dies.

I have modernised the spelling of this tetrastich, which was written by a maternal ancestor of mine who fought for Charles I.*

*   *   *   *   *

Mr. Ruskin has a letter in the *World* newspaper in explanation and defence of his system of publishing. That it is not absolutely perfect is certain ; for I, an admirer of Mr. Ruskin for thirty years, had not the remotest notion how to get a copy of his *Fors Clavigera* till I found a notice of it in a periodical called

---

* It was, of course, his own. Most of the mottoes to the chapters in his novels which he quotes as from various authorities, are his own. The 'Comedy of Dreams,' so often quoted, was never written, though it was, I believe, planned. There are enough fragments of it in the novels to form a large portion of the poem ; and I have had many inquiries from strangers as to where the poem could be found.—F. C.

Cope's Tobacco Plant. Now I had never seen this organ of the smoking world before a friend casually sent it as a curiosity of literature; so, thanks to a perverse method of publication, I get the first news of what our great art critic is doing from a journal for smokers, published in Liverpool! Mr. Ruskin's letter (which, by the way, is not in his choicest English) deserves comment. He says :

'How many authors are strong enough to do without advertisements ?
'None : while advertisement is the practice. But let it become the fashion to announce books once for all in a monthly circular (publisher's, for instance), and the public will simply refer to that for all they want to know. Such advertisement I use now, and always would.'

All very well for an author like Mr. Ruskin, who has never had to live by his pen. I have published just nineteen books, and their being advertised has cost ten times as much as I have got for writing them, and probably twice as much as the publishers got for issuing them. 'Let it become the fashion,' writes Mr. Ruskin, weakly, 'to announce books once for all,' etc. Why, he is strong enough to make the fashion. Why does he not establish a critical journal of a pure and lofty type, which shall record, with an impartiality and skill unknown to our present literary journals, what is done by the wielders of the pen?

* * * * *

In a village where I have been known to sojourn there has recently been placed a clock in the church spire. It is the gift of the heir of a noble old gentleman who calmly trod the paths of life for ninety years, and is dedicated to his memory. Yet on the face of that clock, in huge letters, stands the not unusual name—

SMITH,

that being the patronymic of the clockmaker. Why does this legend glare upon us through the trees? Is it an advertisement purely? Does Smith expect anyone who drives by and admires that dial to order a church clock by return of post? The architect's name is not on the church: why should the clockmaker's name obtrude itself in that aggressive fashion? 'I pause for a reply.'

June 22.

Strolling last Sunday through the churchyard of Waltham St. Lawrence, in Berkshire, I came across the tombstone of the famous John Newbery, bookseller and patent medicine vendor, of St. Paul's Churchyard, who engaged Goldsmith to write for him at the magnificent salary of a hundred a year, and to whom Johnson sold 'The Vicar of Wakefield' for sixty pounds, when its author was arrested by his landlady for arrears of rent. For him Goldsmith wrote children's books; among them 'The History of Little Goody Two Shoes, otherwise Mistress Margery Two Shoes, with the means by which she acquired learning and wisdom, and, in consequence thereof, her estate, set forth at large for the benefit of those

> 'Who from a state of rags and care,
> And having shoes but half a pair,
> Their fortune and their fame should fix,
> And gallop in a coach and six.'

In the vault of John Newbery are buried others members of his family. There is a curious error of dates in the inscription. He is recorded to have died in 1767, aged 34; his daughter Mary in 1792, aged 50, so that she was born in 1742, when he could (according to the inscription) have been only nine years old! As the tomb bears marks of restoration, I suspect the graver's chisel went wrong somewhere at the time, changing perhaps a 5 into a 3 in the publisher's own age.

Here is a portion of his epitaph, exactly as arranged and punctuated:

> 'Stay, Passenger, and contemplate.
> Virtues, which arose on this spot;
> Urbanity, that adorned Society,
> Knowledge, that discerned and
>   Skill, that introduced
> The most powerful discovery
> In the annals of medicine
> The humble wisdom that taught
> And still teaches moral lessons
>   To the rising generation,
>   Lament
> That a breast inspired with such virtues
>   Is sunk in dust.'

I believe 'the most powerful discovery in the annals of medicine' was a worm-powder for children—while of course his child's picture-books were the 'moral lessons.' Compare these stilted phrases with the epitaph on a tomb that lies in the deep shadow of the Temple Church :

<blockquote>'Here lies Oliver Goldsmith.'</blockquote>

June 24.

Nine months have passed since I recorded the death of my faithful little Skye terrier Fido, and now his old companion Growl lies beside him beneath the limes. He was born at Wandsworth, in September, 1862, so he has had a fairly long life for a little dog. I was present at his birth, and christened him Growl, because his first act was to growl at his mother for bringing him into the world without his leave. Poor old boy, he has growled through life, always most at those he loved best, as is the way with some human cynics; and when he let me touch him without growling I knew he was in a bad way. A lion was a coward to the little fellow; he would have attacked one without hesitation. I have known him spring from a boat on the Thames to do battle with an angry male swan in the breeding time, when a black retriever in the boat cowered with terror. He has walked with me through many counties of England, sometimes doing forty miles a day with ease; and once, when walking through Buckinghamshire, we met Mr. and Mrs. Disraeli and just such another little dog in the Hughenden lane, and, although neither he nor I had been introduced, he commenced a conversation at once. That night we stayed at the 'George' at Aylesbury, where I amazed the waiter by eating seven consecutive mutton chops, Growl devouring the bones. Ay, we have had joyous times together, poor little dog; and it is satisfactory to know that, while you shared my gaiety, you had no share in those multitudinous troubles to which man is born.

There is great delight in pilgrimages through England, as Chaucer showed in the verse of England's daybreak. Two young ladies, friends of mine, are coming seventy miles to see me in a few days, in a lady's dog-cart drawn by their famous pony Moonface. They will pass from within sight of Warwick Castle to a distant view of Windsor's stately towers in three days. Do they dread adventures? No; they hope for them: but giants have nearly all perished out of the earth, and those left behind are weak in the knees; and the Knight Errant is gone upon the Stock Exchange; and the Troubadour writes for *Punch;* and even the courteous highwayman, like Claude du Val, who let a lady go unplundered when she had danced a minuet with him, is a pale phantom of the past. Ghosts fled from the wayside inns, like rats from a sinking ship, when the mail-coaches stopped; so I fear my *sorores audaces* will arrive here quite safely, without having even been frightened. Still there is no knowing. Let us hope that the poetry of life is not wholly extinct, and that they may meet with some delightfully dangerous adventure at the picturesque inn known as 'Hopcroft's Holt.'

June 29.

Where are the pretty haymakers of days gone by? The other day I was in the very heart of fragrant hayfields, where my friend Lazy Lawrence has a quiet crib, and reminiscences of my youth returned to me, and I remembered merry innocent romps with gay girls who thought haymaking fun. Your farmers' daughters are above that sort of thing nowadays. Female haymakers I beheld, but, like Wordsworth's fishwomen, they were

'Withered, grotesque, immeasurably old.'

Twenty years have passed—how the years *do* pass, to be sure!—since I wrote, in the July number of the *Dublin University Magazine*, some verses called 'The Amateur Haymakers.' Out of about a hundred lines, one, I venture to think, is good,—

'We Goths have changed the gods of the old Greek faith to gases.'

Considering that Huxley and Tyndall had not at that time come much to the front, I take credit to myself for a kind of prophetic instinct—a fore-feeling of the imminent materialism which turns Apollo into oxygen and Neptune into hydrogen. But now for the haymaking:

> 'They toss the hay-wreaths in the liquid air;
> They chase each other; merry children, fair
> As if this earth had never known a stain,
> Sing many a pleasant carol,
> Weave ruddy flower apparel:
> Surely the days return of Saturn's peaceful reign.'

That was in 1855. I don't see anything of the kind in 1875. The young girls of the present day are too 'swell' to toss the hay about. They were making hay in a picturesque hillside orchard, near which my friend took me. 'Look at that,' quoth Lawrence the Lotos-eater.

I looked. It was a girl of fourteen or so, with her hair dressed in tails with ribbon ties, like the Miss Kenwigses in 'Nicholas Nickleby.' She was seated amid the hay, tying up bundles of flowers and looking lackadaisical.

'Hast thou a moral, my friend?' I said, knowing that Lazy Lawrence has a philosophic mind.

'Well, not much,' he replied. 'But that dressed-up chit is the daughter of a small farmer and publican—though perhaps *small* is not the proper word for him. And you should hear her murder music on a wretched piano in his little inn. Why can't people of that class have sense enough to teach their children something useful? She is growing up to think herself a lady—and there are hundreds of such cases.'

Lawrence gets very angry over this kind of thing. Although nothing will induce him to work himself (and as he need not, why should he?), he is very hard on people who won't work. On this occasion, less lazy than usual, he improvised a parody on some rare old lines:

> 'Man, till your soil,
> Wife, think and toil,
> Boy, dig and hoe,
> Girl, knit and sew,
>   And you'll keep your true level.
> Man, drive a pair,
> Wife, satin wear,
> Boy, smoke and swill,
> Girl, have your will,
>   And you'll go to . . . .'

Need I say where? The rhyme settles the

point. My friend Lawrence has his peculiarities, but his rhymes are usually all right.

July 1.

I have just been reading a translation, by Mr. Davenport Adams, of some notes by Sainte-Beuve in his 'Nouveaux Lundis' on the Gospel of St. Matthew. The French essayist, famed for subtlety and style, failed to understand the simple Evangelist. Quoting the Beatitudes, he sagely remarks that 'undoubtedly some obscurities mingle with the mild lights which issue from these words.' I do not know, as the French is not before me, what the original of 'mild lights' may be; but it seems to me that those few words of Christ's are the very essence of religion, and are in themselves enough to prove His absolute inspiration. They are utterly devoid of obscurity, and they throw a light stronger than the sun's at noon on the paradoxes of human existence. Sainte-Beuve is perplexed on the threshold by πτωχοί τῷ πνεύματι, very well translated as 'poor in spirit.' He wonders whether the phrase means 'poor in goods,' or 'poor in ideas.' Assuredly not.

The poor in spirit are they who, having real spiritual strength, use it humbly and modestly —and theirs is the Kingdom of Heaven. They are kings on earth already. Every line of the Sermon on the Mount is full of divine light, and the strong simplicity of the pregnant sentences perplexes the modern French essayist. The Evangelists were not 'perfect and precise writers,' says Sainte-Beuve. There is nothing more perfect and precise in all literature than Christ's Sermon on the Mount as reported in the Gospels. Careless readers, appreciating its beauty and poetry, fail to perceive that it is strictly scientific. The keynote of it is, 'Be ye therefore perfect, even as your Father, which is in Heaven, is perfect.' Here an absolute impossibility is prescribed, as indeed throughout the whole Sermon. Therein is the unique scientific beauty of that ever-memorable discourse, caught up by a few fishermen to form the creed of Christendom. Open Euclid. 'A point is that which hath no parts, or which hath no magnitude. A line is length without breadth.' Has any man ever seen Euclid's point or Euclid's line? Yet they are imaginable; and even so, imaginable but unattainable, is the perfection of which Christ spoke. The Sermon on the Mount is not only the most beautiful of religious discourses; it is also a very profound scientific treatise on theology. In this latter aspect it has been neglected, and I do not think we shall get much aid in its investigation from French *littérateurs*. Take the great saying, μὴ μεριμνᾶτε τῆς ψυχῆς ὑμῶν—'take no thought for your life.' It appears to me that a man like Sainte-Beuve could not understand its deep significance. It means that mere life here, the indwelling of the soul in the body, is a thing to be considered trivial in comparison with what a man has to do, if he does his duty. Go straight; perish as hero or martyr, or man unknown; there is the world beyond—not another, but the same.[*]

---

[*] Mortimer Collins certainly carried out this precept himself, for although he had the power of both physical and mental enjoyment to the highest degree, he never feared death. He seemed to have perfect confidence in a life beyond the present, and the prospect of 'shuffling off the mortal coil' gave him no alarm. He very prettily expresses

Sainte-Beuve prattles about 'innocent and virginal images.' Frenchmen are a queer mixture of the tiger and the baby; but there are few stronger sayings than this—οὐ δύνασθε Θεῷ δουλεύειν καὶ μαμμωνᾳ. A good many people in the present day *do* imagine that a reconciliation between God and Mammon is possible; but they will discover their mistake in time.

his ideas on this subject in a poem on 'Sleep,' three stanzas of which are perhaps worth quoting.

> Is life a dream, and death a sleep, and love
>   The only thing immortal ? Who would care
>   To be received into the ambient air,
> Or traverse æther like a cloud, above
>   The happy homes of mortals ? Must the soul
>   Be formlessly absorbed into the infinite whole ?
>
> No : I shall pass into the Morning Land
>   As now from sleep into the life of morn ;
>   Live the new life of the new world, unshorn
> Of the swift brain, the executing hand ;
>   See the dense darkness suddenly withdrawn,
>   As when Orion's sightless eyes discerned the dawn.
>
> I shall behold it : I shall see the utter
>   Glory of sunrise heretofore unseen,
>   Freshening the woodland ways with brighter green,
> And calling into life all wings that flutter,
>   All throats of music and all eyes of light,
>   And driving o'er the verge the intolerable night.

Meanwhile I should recommend them to study the Sermon on the Mount without the help of a dexterous and possibly sinister French essayist.

July 6.

I was sorry, the other day, to hear that an old friend of mine had been for some years dead. I met a procession of vans, one of which was drawn by dromedaries, its driver being a very melancholy man. Driving dromedaries is melancholy work, I fancy. It was Edmond's Menagerie (late Wombwell's, I may observe) on its travels. I asked the melancholy dromedary-driver about a blind tiger in which I felt an affectionate interest. When that tiger came over to England he had to be slightly touched with a red-hot poker before he would enter his cage. Then, by some strange accident, he walked out into the Ratcliffe Highway, and was about to eat a boy, when Mr. Jamrach interfered with his enjoyment by knocking him on the head with a heavy bar of iron. From that time he was blind; but when I last saw him, nearly twenty years ago, he had just killed a promising young lion, breaking through the iron wires of his cage to do it. That tiger is dead. Will no one join me in a sentimental tear?

One of the huge vans came to grief on the roadside. Luckily no carnivorous creatures got loose; but I was much amused at the calm philosophy with which a couple of elephants employed the time in eating the hedge foliage, and at the intense curiosity with which the small boys and girls watched the elephants. That incident will be an epoch in some infantile lives. Had a tiger strayed out and picked up a baby it would have been more impressive. My father was outside the coach on Salisbury Plain (at Winterslow, I think), when a lioness that had escaped from a menagerie attacked the horses, and was shot by the guard. A bull-dog flew at the brute, and was killed if I remember aright. The railway has put an end to such picturesque adventures. If a stray lion or tiger were to attack an express train, there would be very little of him left afterwards. Yet unperceiving the forgetive force which makes man monarch of the world, doth not Darwin maintain that we are developed from the lower creatures? Strange blindness and love of paradox!

CHAPTER V.

1875. JULY AND AUGUST.

We've removed the political blister ;
And Wyndham, whose wife and whose sister
    Are charming, has taken a moor :
He writes, ' You must rough it, old fellow ;
This box with old age has grown mellow,
    But I hope you won't think it a bore.'

A bore ! In the first place, there's Wyndham—
There are no jolly sins but he's sinn'd 'em ;
    He's always in love or in debt.
Than his wife there's no beauty that's blonder ;
But perchance of gay Jessy I'm fonder —
    A mischievous merry brunette.

That shooting-box, worse for the weather
Of years, nested snug amid heather,
    With a beck tripping noisily by,—
I have known it three capital seasons,
And have given three excellent reasons
    Why thither from London I fly.

But if Wyndham, his lady, and Jessy,
Wild-witty and daintily dressy,
   Suffice not your critical nous,
This reason, O friend and O brother,
I give you a fourth, yea another—
   That moor has abundance of grouse.

O joyous the luncheon at noon is,
When languor conducive to spoon is!
   The ladies on ponies come up,
And bring us cold birds and flirtation—
Combined, a delightful sensation,
   With really miraculous cup.

Then at night the half-dinner, half-supper;
And Jessy sings songs (out of Tupper,
   It may be, or possibly mine),
And cavendish lends its aroma;
And laziness, lotos, and coma
   Make the heart of the Highlands divine.

Dear Editor, he is the true sage
Who of happy occasions makes usage,
   Selecting Time's loveliest gems:
Perhaps I'm as snug in the Highlands
As you where the willow-crown'd islands
   Break full-flowing current of Thames.

July 8.

BURNHAM BEECHES is a lovely bit of forest ground: few such spots are there in England: I was there this week, in company of very pleasant ladyhood: a naval officer had promised to join us, but missed his train, and missed also an uncommonly good lobster. By that lobster there hangs a tale. Most picnics have some kind of difficulty. I have known the hamper of wine forgotten. I have also known a picnic without a corkscrew; but that has never happened since with me. I never go anywhere without a penknife and a corkscrew. But our lobster! It came down from London to the Bear Hotel at Maidenhead, with other matters, such as pine-apples and strawberries, which help to make a picnic pleasant; but when we opened the basket, we found that lobster was not boiled! However, Mr. Dawson, as amiable a host as ever lived, sent it into the kitchen, and we started twenty minutes later than we had intended, Astacus hot from his pot.

Do my readers know Burnham Beeches? Do they know Luttrel, poet and wit? He wrote a charming little poem on the grand old beech forest, and there is this week in *Punch* some verse in the same metre, suggested by Mr. Vernon Heath the photographer's letter to the *Times*, mourning the fall of the Monarch

Beech. Luttrel is very happy in some of his stanzas, and most of those who know the old forest-fragment will echo his wish :

> O ne'er may woodman's axe resound,
> Nor tempest, making breaches,
> In the sweet shade that cools the ground,
> Beneath our Burnham Beeches.

However, the tempest will do its devastating work. Mr. Vernon Heath's letter in the *Times* suggested the verses in *Punch* which I have mentioned, which are in Luttrel's metre, and which by odd accident I read this week beneath one of the giants of Burnham.* The grand old wood was rather cockneyfied. I don't think I ever saw it so haunted by ponies, donkeys, and *canaille*. It seemed almost as bad as 'Ampstead 'Eath. When you want to sit quietly beneath a noble tree in a forest such as Arden might have been, and to enjoy a pleasant time with ladies of the fairest forms, and cavaliers who have something poetic about

---

* We have already quoted verses on Burnham Beeches, by Mortimer Collins in the previous chapter. Those alluded to here were also by him.—F. C.

them, it really is no joke to have an audience of dirty children around you. To do the children justice, though water had not touched their cuticles for a long period, they were not offensive, and they divided the eatables we gave them in a generous way. They did not act in the spirit of the greedy boy in 'Original Poems':

> 'I've got a plum cake, and a rare feast I'll make,
> I'll eat, and I'll stuff, and I'll cram.'

Still, I would rather sit beneath those grand trees without a heap of small children at hand, without the idle fellows who lend ponies and donkeys. A grey-haired clergyman was there, with a quiver full of youngsters, whom he put on donkeys, and they quite enjoyed it. Yet, if I had the pleasure of his acquaintance, I should have felt disposed to inquire whether children on donkeys were quite in place under the most glorious beeches to be found in England. I like to see a little girl on a donkey; but there are many places where chits may have their donkey-rides without vulgarising the august sanctity of a forest.

July 15.

Saint Swithin! A thousand and fourteen years ago, sometime in July, his *lic* (old English for corpse) was laid in Winchester churchyard, by his own desire. He wished the sun to shine and the rain to rain upon his grassy grave. But there were others who deemed the great bishop deserved higher honour; so they built a golden shrine in the cathedral, and wished to remove his body thereto, and were delayed by forty days of the heaviest rain ever known. Such the old tradition, on which is built the superstition indicated in the following rhyme :

> ' Saint Swithin's Day, if thou dost rain,
> For forty days it will remain ;
> Saint Swithin's Day, if thou be fair,
> For forty days it will rain na mair.

I cannot quite understand the Scottish form of the last line, since it relates to a Bishop of the Kingdom of Wessex. Should it rain for forty days from this Saint Swithin—*videlicet*, to Saint Bartholomew—there will be no wheat harvest in England. Even now the wheat fields are looking as if a heavy roller had been passed over them. It is a saddening sight, for we know what hardship falls upon the poor at times when harvests are ruined. As to the customary garden-parties of July, they for the most part have collapsed entirely. Cricket matches have had to be played in a swamp. Mulled claret and soda negus have superseded Badminton and gin-sling. We 'breathe in converse seasons,' as Mr. Tennyson, with his customary quaintness, puts it. Our dear friends in Australia are having their winter, and so are we; but it is perhaps hardly fair that *we* should have two winters in the year, when *they* don't. However, there are creatures who seem greatly to enjoy it. At this moment starlings and blackbirds and thrushes are tugging away at the worms on my lawn with unusual success. Whether the worms like it or not, the result is feathered music, delighting human ears. Worms were designed to be eaten by birds, and will suffer that treatment through all time, unless Mr. Darwin can induce them to develop into something else. Why should he not? If an ascidian becomes an ape, and an ape a man, there ought to be no difficulty about a worm's becoming a boa constrictor, and defying the birds. There is a female blackbird now within my ken feeding four little ones (her second brood of four this year) with indefatigable assiduity.

*   *   *   *   *

Do my readers suffer from the plague of impertinent letter-writing? The advertising tradesfolk are bad enough, with their sherry that will cure the gout (I haven't the gout, and touch no sherry), and their quack medicines that will cure everything, and their sales of invaluable articles at a loss, and a thousand other devices to catch flats. *Obiter dictum:* never buy of a tradesman who is always advertising; you will have to help to pay him for his advertisements. Then there are the charity-seekers, who want to send flannel shirts to Central Africa, or to get an orphan (poor little wretch! let's hope they'll fail) into an asylum, or to build a church in some deserted district. I think, if English Churchmen hold their own and forget their divisions, wherever a church is needed it will build itself. But your worst fiend is the anonymous letter-writer. Holding decided opinions, and having (who coined the phrase?) the courage of my opinions, I have in my time printed things which other people did not like. Well, I see in the papers a great many things I don't like, but I write no letters to their authors. Thought is free. Every man has a right to utter his mind. I shall certainly utter mine, so long as I have power to do it adequately.

July 16.

Why, oh why, did I write of fine weather last week? It has rained pertinaciously ever since. That enthusiastic agriculturist, Mr. Mechi, who was born to falsify Virgil's exclamation:

' O fortunati agricolae, sua si bona norint!'

has found a proverb that praises 'a dripping June.' Is there one in favour of a dripping July? If not, let us make one:

A dripping July
Is good for the fly:

not the turnip fly, Mr. Mechi, but the fly on four wheels. Or, turn the rhyme round, and say :

>July that is damp
>Makes us relish the 'gamp'—

whereby I mean that useful umbrella of rough material, the great-grandmother of which was carried by the amiable old lady whom Dickens has immortalised. Just now, however, July is neither damp nor dripping—it pours, as I have reason to know, having just come home wet through, so thoroughly soaked that even that best tempered of Good Templars, Sir Wilfrid, would allow me one glass of whisky, medicinally. So I present Mr. Mechi with one more couplet :

>July, when it pours
>Is the dreariest of bores.

If any of my innumerable readers has influence with that fickle functionary, the clerk of the weather, I do hope he or she will use it. The state of affairs is alarming. A member of the Atmospherical Society whom I happen to know tells me it is all because the Tories are in office. I ought perhaps to mention that he is also a member of the Cromwell Commonwealth Club.

*   *   *   *   *

I have not seen 'The Papers of a Critic,' selected from the writings of the late Charles Wentworth Dilke, and edited by his grandson and namesake, whom everybody who knows cannot help liking for his frankness and fairness, though perchance widely differing (as I do) from his opinions. But in *Notes and Queries* of the 10th, there is quoted from the book a lovely letter from father to son on his birthday, full of real tenderness and wise advice—a model letter. A man with such a father could hardly fail to be a man of mark. There is a little sermon on this text: 'I do not desire to have you a great Latin scholar .... but I do wish you to know and understand Latin as well as you do English.' I will not quote Mr. Dilke's illustrations of the value of such knowledge—everybody will read the book. But I hope the strong opinion on this point of an impartial thinker and careful critic will have some weight against the crazes of modern school-board reformers, with their 'ologies and 'ographics and 'isms. If to know Latin were only to know Horace and Virgil, it would be an efficient education. If it were also to know Cicero and Cæsar, it would give a grand apparatus of intellectual power. These are few names. Having the great authority of Mr. Dilke to sustain me, I say that to leave a boy of fair intellect, who will not have to live by manual labour, untrained in Latin, is most unfair to him. Of Greek I say nothing just at present, as the modern scientific certificated schoolmaster seems to shy at the alphabet of that language.

* * * * *

July 22.

Do you like tortoises, gentle reader? They are not lively. I have had one on my lawn now for some years—there were two originally, but the other was of a restless condition, and after making several excursions, at one time being absent for months, has vanished entirely. It is curious to watch their tranquil torpid life. They take existence easily: they fear not lightning or thunder; they are incapable of being attacked by ordinary enemies; when the cold comes, they bury themselves in the ground and sleep through the winter. Two legends have the Greeks of the tortoise, which show that the world's most agile-minded life-watching race looked on the creature with interest. In the Homeric Hymn to Hermes, we find the inventive son of Maïa springing from his cradle on the day of his birth (mercurial infant!), crossing the threshold, seeing a tortoise, and at once divining that it was the very creature to transmute into an instrument of music. So the baby-deity exclaimed (I use Shelley's translation):

> 'A youthful godsend are you to me now,
> King of the dance, companion of the feast,
> Lovely in all your nature.'

And he scooped out the luckless tortoise with scalpel of steel, and stretched seven concordant strings of sheep, and lo, the lyre! Good work for a babe just born; especially as at once he began to sing, with lyric accompaniment, the whole romantic story of the amour of his father and mother. Thus got we the *grata testudo* of Horace. In another old Greek story the reptile had its revenge upon a poet. Æschylus, ninety years old, was meditating by the sea : an eagle, that had clutched a tortoise, and wanted to crack its shell, flew high in air, and dropped it right on the immortal poet's bald pate. There was an end of the author of ' Prometheus Bound.' The proceedings of the coroner's inquest are not extant, else we might discover whether that eagle was trying an experiment to ascertain the thickness of a poet's skull.

* * * * *

The Clothworkers' Company are liberal. I notice in one number of the *Times* scholarships endowed by them for the Royal Naval School and for Girton College, Cambridge. Girton is a ladies' college, and promises to be a success. 'Tis all very well to laugh at strong-minded women and blue-stockings; but I never met with a woman who knew a little of classical literature (even through translations) or of geometry who was not improved thereby. One lady I know whose native geometry makes her a capital architect—as you would say if you saw her additions to a country cottage I know of. I think Sir Arthur Helps, in one of his earliest works, dwells on the value of geometry to ladies. I agree with him. It is the loveliest of abstract sciences; and few studies are more charming than the sections of the cone, geometrically considered. But I can't for the life of me see why ladies should not read Homer and Horace, except, perhaps, that there is no one to teach them. How much more would they learn from the Bible of Greece and the poet-philosopher of Rome than from the twaddle of 'Télémaque!' At the same time, they should read English— good sound strong sterling English such as our ancestors wrote—prose with the thrust of the rapier and verse with the ring of the nightingale in it.

July 29.

Dr. Newman says there are two ideas of God—one as a moral governor and judge, the other as the centre of that immense machine, the Universe. I do not quote Dr. Newman's exact words, but this is the sense of them. Why do people split hairs when they have analogy to guide them? Cannot the Creator of a myriad worlds, the Orderer of all events, be a Mind as well as a machine? Analyse yourself, my friend. You are a machine, just like the universe; but are you wholly unconscious of something subtle and volatile which is the controller of that machine? You are not a mere automaton. The spirit breathed into you is a part of the infinite Creative Spirit. It is astounding to see two schools, Spiritualist and Materialist, fighting for ever about the question of a Creator, or a chaos becoming cosmos by chance, when a man's inborn thought should enable him to see that mind creates matter, and that without mind matter would be impossible.

Aug. 5.

White rats seem the fashion; I don't mean political white rats. I hear of them from all quarters. I bought a couple a day or two ago, and hope to study their peculiarities. Few animals that I have tried are so pretty in their habits or so charmingly tame. They lie on the palm of a lady's hand, and play tricks with her finger-nails. Their frolics in a cage (the larger the better) are delightful. It is my first introduction to these charming quadrumanous creatures, and I am marvellously pleased with them. Their instinctive tameness and fearlessness are wonderful. When a Pyrenean wolfhound and a Gordon setter walked up to investigate their cage, they put their pink noses through the wires and regarded their invaders without the slightest sign of alarm.

Aug. 12.

Talking of character, I am reminded of a saying, which I think is Goethe's, that 'Character is destiny.' This, doubtless, is a partial truth. A man's character is a determining force. You may compare the saying, erroneously attributed to Bacon, that 'Knowledge is power;' whereas knowledge is merely an element of power. Byron was a man of very small knowledge, but he had a hundred times the power of Robert Browning, who is plusquam-omniscient—whose knowledge is *de omni scibile, et quibusdam aliis*. Compare the knowledge of Gladstone with the knowledge of Palmerston: which had the greatest power? Friedrich von Hardenberg, writing under the *nom de plume* of Novalis, ventured on the aphorism that 'Character ought to be greater than destiny,' of which saying the poet Coleridge approved. And surely, in every man who aspires there are certain possibilities which never (on this planet) become realities; just as the skylark climbs the infinite stair of heaven to bear his song to the door of the Empyrean Palace, and each day, as his wings grow stronger and his note clearer, he comes closer to the jasper gates, and each day, baffled by his toil of upward travel, he flutters back to his nest amid the dewy grass, saddened by inevitable failure, yet

'True to the kindred points of Heaven and Home.'

Now, this seems just what men are compelled

to do who have a sublime ideal. I believe not in the 'Village Hampden,' and 'mute inglorious Milton' of the poet Gray, morbidly mooning in Stoke Pogis churchyard, and composing an elegy so invertebrate in its character that the lines, and the words in the lines, can be changed without injury to the sense. With Coleridge, I prefer the opinion of Novalis to that of Goethe. And the reason is clear. Character is designed to develop, not on the surface of this planet only, but elsewhere, in space and time to us unimaginable. What a man does here is the likelier to be less than what he might do, in exact ratio with his innate power. Great genius wants ample elbow-room. I have recently been looking through a ridiculous book by a Frenchman, Figuier, who fixes the precise future of everybody, and puts good people in the sun. Well, as the sun is in volume just 360,000 times the size of the earth, there ought to be ample space, and vast palaces, and spacious gardens for all the really good people we have produced for many generations. Still I am not one of those who think the indestructible spirit of man is to find interminable ease and rest in a kind of fools' paradise. The soul being immortal, it must always move and grow, expanding in the infinite universe which the Creator has provided for it.

The monarch beech of Burnham Beeches was blown down a month or two ago: a fact notified in the *Times* by our great landscape photographer, Mr. Vernon Heath, who had photographed it as a representative of Autumn in his series of the four seasons in the beech-forest, and subsequently turned into an elegy by Mr. *Punch*. Mr. Heath has just sent me a photograph on a grand scale of this gnarled veteran, and I take the occasion to recommend everybody to buy a copy—but especially those who have cut their own initials or their sweetheart's on the bark, for the letters come out beautifully. The way in which the interlacing boughs are given—the aerial effect—is a triumph of photographic art. By the way, it is a noteworthy indication of what we have had to call summer this year, that Mr. Vernon Heath travelled a thousand miles in search of

Thoughts in my Garden.

lovely scenery to photograph—and never once unpacked his apparatus!

Aug. 17.

The world is on the wing. On the breezy moors of Scotland sportsmen are trudging manfully after the grouse, and coming home in the twilight to their shooting-boxes with grand appetites and sound digestions. To all the sea-side places there is one continued pilgrimage; and we mourn that we have no longer Leech to sketch the mermaids who let down their ravishing back hair to dry in the soft south wind. There may be other men as good; yet it seems as if no one ever had such a healthy delight in depicting the trim-ankled nymphs who find renewal of beauty in the many-twinkling tide whence the Goddess of Beauty arose, and who, like the sea-birds of Cayster, love

'To wanton in the luxury of splash,'

as Mr. Blackmore translates Virgil. Well, London is rapidly emptying itself of the merry maidens of the present day, with all their eccentricities—

> The girls who love Darwin and Tyndall,
>   The girls who love polo and rink ;
> The girls whom our Gladstone can kindle
>   And cause them to think that they think ;
> The girls who are nice and who know it,
>   The girls who are nicer, and don't,
> The girls who will flirt with a poet,
>   The girls who are wiser, and won't :
> The gaiety's past, and the passion ;
>   From ballrooms the mad music dies,
> And we wait for next summer's new fashion
>   In petticoats, tresses, and eyes.

It always seems to me a pity that so few of the young ladies of the present day learn to read. ' Don't learn to read ?' exclaims Miss Angelina Pinnock, schoolmistress after the newest lights, who teaches all the 'ologies, and physics her elder girls with salts and senna when they fancy themselves in love. ' Why, they learn to read be-utifully, and there isn't a girl among them that can't spell *valetudinarian* and *antitrinitarian*. What does the irreverent man mean ?'

Well, it may seem a paradox, but I like a paradox now and then. That word ' paradox' does not mean something untrue, but something contrary to vulgar opinion. Now, in this sense, I maintain that girls are seldom taught to read; for by learning to read I mean learning *what* to read, *how* to read it, *when* and *where* to read it. I remember being struck by a story of the poet Coleridge. He was staying by the seaside, and a friend went to see him. He found the poet on the 'ribbed sea sand,' with a noble sunset colouring the hyaline; he was leading one of his boys—a mere child—and reciting to him passages from the 'Odyssey.' When that youngster came to read Homer, how he would associate the song of the Syrens and the story of Nausikaa with the long sea-like roll of the dactylics he had heard his father declaiming by the unconquered demesne of Ennosigaios!

I suppose it would be ridiculous to counsel young ladies to read Homer by the sea, even in the Earl of Derby's translation; yet I fancy they would find it furnish more food to the mind than the frivolous novels which are now sold by myriads at the railway stations. Think of reading 'Lady Audley's Secret,' or 'Cometh up as a Flower,' or the prolusions of

'Mrs. Brown,' when the great ocean is moving endlessly beneath the travelling winds. Then is the time for the third canto of 'Childe Harold,' or for Shakespeare's 'Tempest.' 'Oh,' cries Miss Angelina Pinnock, 'you wicked man! I have taught all my young ladies that Shakespeare is improper, and Byron even worse:' and *that* the modern schoolmistress calls teaching children to read; whereas it is teaching them *not* to read. Boys at the public schools get acquainted, whether they like it or not, with

> 'The glory that was Greece,
> And the grandeur that was Rome;'

but girls, with their mere smattering of modern languages, read nothing of much better quality than such rubbish as 'Télémaque.' Hence, never having entered the higher domains of English literature, when they begin to want something to read, they are taken by the latest new novel, with its impossible situations, unreal characters, and slangy style. So I return to my thesis: they have not learnt to read. Imagine the delight of reading the 'Tempest,' in those great caves of Sark, which open to the sea wide portals, tapestried with myriad-coloured sea-anemones, like the palace of a sea deity, the boudoir of Argorupeza—whom Zeus loved but dared not wed because the fates had willed her son should be greater than his sire! Imagine 'As You Like It' under the oaks of Stoneleigh or the beeches of Burnham.

But the young ladies of the present time assure you that they don't read poetry. Precisely. A person who cannot read poetry has not learnt to read, for that is the very essence of reading—'the best words in the best order,' as Coleridge briefly defined it. Our young ladies pretend to admire Tennyson because he is the fashion: make anything the fashion, from Ritualism to rat-catching, and the fashionable world will run after it, like sheep after the bell-wether. What would you say of a man who professed to read Latin, yet could make nothing of Horace? The silly novels which infatuate our illiterate female children are devoid of all intellectual stimulus: no thought, no form, no style. They bear about the same resemblance to real literature as shandygaff to dry champagne, or a pie made from that noble animal the cat to the artistic *patisserie* of Périgord. And this shower of nonsense is eagerly received by the pupils of Miss Angelina Pinnock and her rivals—because they have never learnt to read.

Aug. 19.

The vicissitudes of literary fashion are curious. It has been observed that the Athenian drama, in its way the most perfect triumph of dramatic art, lasted only about a hundred years. A notable article in the *Saturday Review* some few weeks ago pointed out the impossibility of anything like the Elizabethan drama being renewed in England. In those days readers were few. The people were taught orally. They got their politics from preachers at Paul's Cross; their history from William Shakespeare. They were stirring times, when the greatness of England lay on the hazard of a die; and the poetic daring of the fifth

Harry gave stimulus to the people who lived under intrepid Elizabeth. Great translators were introducing to English readers the master works of Greece and Rome; from these Shakespeare, with 'his small Latin and less Greek,' drew largely, and taught men what Agamemnon and Ulysses, Anthony and his 'serpent of Old Nile,' Cæsar and Brutus, would have been if they had had English blood in their veins, for, with all his transcendent magic of local colour, there is always an English touch in the character of his *dramatis personæ*. 'He sent all the old Greeks to school again,' said Coleridge of 'Troilus and Cressida.' To the true lover of Homer, this seems a sacrilege; but it was inevitable, when one man of immense original power took up the theme of another, quite his equal, and living amid the mighty phantoms, and seducing the nymphs of the Pagan Olympus. Catullus caught the spirit of Homer without servile imitation: but Virgil seems very flat when he treads in the old Greek track. Homer's Helen of Troy, the swan-like daughter of Zeus, whose life was the accomplishment of a destiny, begun that day when Peleus wedded Thetis, who had a divinity which severed her from mortal ethics, is a conception as far above Shakespeare's amorous coquette as it is above Mr. Rossetti's nude hetaira. The idea of a fixed fate, against which it is vain to struggle, came from Ægypt into Greece, and ran through mythology, epic, tragedy. It was foreign to Englishmen, an Arminian race, believers in freedom of will.

Agreeing with the writer in the *Saturday* that never again, though we multiply theatres and music-halls, Byrons and Burnands, can we have anything like the Elizabethan drama, since the theatre can never again be the chief source of all secular knowledge, I feel disposed to speculate on the future of the Novel. Is that form of literature likely to last? It is a misfortune that the public, for whom it is written, is a frivolous public, and that not one novel in ten years is a work of art, likely to be read when a generation has passed. The young lady pays her subscription to Mudie, gets her box of books, reads them when she is bored, and likes them much if there is a very naughty hero or a very lachrymose and alluring heroine. As Thackeray's *Pall Mall Gazette* was to be written 'by gentlemen for gentlemen,' so may it be said that most contemporary novels are written by silly girls for silly girls. This depravation of literature can scarcely endure; and, as the absence of a taste for masculine writing, study of character, knowledge of men and books, is likely to prevent writers of real power from trying the Novel, we may predict its decadence in its present form. The library system, the three volume system, and the readiness of second-rate publishers to take any trash they can get cheap, all help towards the inevitable change.

Aug. 26.

People who understand the art of writing are aware that the first condition of success is a good pen-blade; the second, a good quill; the third, brain, to use them both. Your artist in ink cuts his quill quite differently as he may be about to gossip with a friend, or fight an enemy, or woo a lady. So of literature: you want quite different pens for novel, and essay, and lyric. Steel pens are in the main answerable for the stupendous monotony of our modern literature. *Could the afflicting leaders of certain morning papers be written with anything but steel pens?* I trow not. A grey goose quill would gallop away with the writer and produce something so original as to make the sagacious editor's hair stand on end—

'Like quills upon the fretful porcupine.'

*   *   *   *   *

Walking through Amersham some years ago, I noticed an inscription at the end of the village something in this style: 'All vagrants and musicians will be put in the stocks.' Of course I inquired for the stocks, but they had perished long since; and the inscription seemed of a date far before the invasion of organ-grinders. Who were the wandering musicians that peaceful Amersham wisely objected to? I suppose the Amersham of to-day would gladly open its town-hall (if it possesses such an edifice) to the Marquise de Caux, or the Titiens, or Mr. Sims Reeves. Ah, but these are singers, and singers are not always musicians, unluckily. Doubtless the old warning struck at blind fiddlers, players on the Pandean pipe, Welshmen with harps, Scotchmen with bagpipes, Irishmen with patriotic songs and shillelaghs. By the way, if any Parliamentary lover of quiet should bring in a bill against organ-grinders, how would the draughtsman describe those hideous invaders of our peace? *Organ* is a vague word; the *Times* is an organ, and so is the human brain, and so is a chest packed with discord. *Grinder* is quite as dubious; it may mean a Sheffield worker, or a man working hard at his examination, or a tooth, or a knife-grinder. What would be Parliamentary English for organ-grinder?

* * * * *

It was a saying of the Duke of Wellington's that 'habit is ten times stronger than nature.' He was thinking of bad habits, I fancy; but his terse apophthegm is capable of extension to habit of all kinds, and is, in fact, only a familiar way of stating the fact that man is designed to develop himself—and also the world around him. The American boy, who said that 'God made him about ten inches long, and he growed the rest,' was not far from the apprehension of a great truth. When Newton defined genius as only patient labour, he undervalued his own unique power; at the same time he was conscious that he had dwelt laboriously on problem after problem before he had worked them into his great astronomic theory. You carry a philosophic difficulty about with you, and the mind never leaves it; I regret to say that, many a year ago, the solution of a tough philosophical problem burst upon me in the middle of an eloquent sermon from the present Bishop of Peterborough, then curate (I think) of the Octagon Chapel at Bath.

Now, it really is quite worth considering that habit may be cultivated so as to control nature. The most indolent man in the world, if he gets up at six o'clock for a week, will find it easy to go on for a month, and almost impossible after that time to lie in bed till ten. So of the innumerable trifles which make up the sum of human life. It is sad to see how young men in these days think it necessary to drink spirits every evening. The habit, once formed, is hard to conquer; but it is most certain to shorten life. Up to thirty, at least, a man should be able to live without spirits. I allow him whisky in a Scotch mist on a grouse moor, or a gin-sling after an innings of three figures at cricket; but in the latter case a cool tankard of bitter would do him twice the good. Ale, being nutritious as well as stimulant, is the best fluid food for men who take active exercise. But the highest authorities hold that it should be seldom drunk after forty.

I have taken commonplace examples of the formation of habit; but the theory has a very general application. Man is a living spirit, fettered to a perfect machine, which is placed under his control. What we style will is the action of the spirit of man on the machine aforesaid. The first time it is driven a reverse way the machine is troublesome; thus, if you have been taking hot baths for months, your first cold bath will take your breath away. Persevere, you will soon enjoy the cold water, and shrink from the notion of a hot bath. So a miserable man who looks at the seamy side of life, may, if he uses his will, get a glimpse of the sunny side, and the glimpse will grow brighter daily till it expands into full vision. So the man who shudders at the sight of a book, and would walk twenty miles to avoid a metaphysician, were he resolutely to read an hour a day, would be rapturously exclaiming with Milton (a borrower from Shakespeare):

> 'How charming is divine Philosophy!
> Not harsh and crabbed as dull fools suppose,
> But musical as is Apollo's lute.'

CHAPTER VI.

AUTUMN, 1875.

Ay, the gay time is here,
Sweetest of all the year,
Cool be the bitter beer,
   Straight be the cartridge.
Session and season o'er,
Girl-flirt and Statesman-bore,
Seek we the joyous shore,
   Worship Saint Partridge.

Horace, that demirep
(Known as a fifth form step),
Sang of the quiet *Sep-*
   tembribus horis:
And it appears to me,
Even by land or sea,
This month must surely be
   Mensis amoris.

Yes, when the toil is o'er,
When we forget the bore,
Then, by some happy shore,
   Quiet the pulse is:
Far from the City's fuss
Bright eyes rain joy on us,
Deep woods are glorious—
   Latebræ dulces.

D., who would catch the tide,
G., with his notions wide,
Each is temporicide—
   Time's reckless murderer:
Past now; the moon is bright
O'er sea and sand to-night;
Lady, with dainty sleight,
   Ice me the Rœderer.

Confound their politics!
Plague on their knavish tricks!
Doubtless, in Seventy-Six,
   Stalks some fresh spectre in.
But 'tis September now;
Far off be any row;
Sea-breezes cool my brow—
   Hand me a nectarine.

               Sept. 2.

SEPTEMBER is here, and everybody is wandering everywhere. Yachts dance upon the Solent; pretty girls let down their back hair on Dawlish sands, with, alas! no Leech to sketch them as they chatter and laugh under the red rocks; lovers of sport trudge over their own 'turmuts;' lovers of fashion go to Trouville and Deanville, and wear a new dress every day, and pay ten times its value for all they eat and drink. Why not stay at home? This I ask, not of the Londoner, but the man who has green grass and shady trees of his own. September seems to me the last month wherein to desert your lares and penates. Brighton toward the end of October, when the country grows bare and desolate, is not unpleasant; it gives one a fillip, that sea that seems always fretted by the wind, that gay, grotesque society which includes all possible classes. Were you ever at a ball at the Grand Hotel, dear reader, or at a late supper of authors, artists, and actors at the Old Ship? A quaint contrast—Jewesses, diamonded, and fair Greeks and millionaire stockbrokers at the one; and, in the old days, Dickens and Mark Lemon and Buckstone at the other. Comparisons are odious, so I will not say where the wine was soundest, where the wit most radiant.

But in September, if a man has got a home, he should stay in it. The Venusian's happy hexameters ring in my ears :

> 'Hae latebrae dulces, etiam, si credis, amoenae,
>   Incolumem tibi me praestant Septembribus horis.'

It seems to me the very time of all the year for home delight. How long the shadows in the brisk, fresh morning, when you hear the starlings talk wisely on the roof, and see blackbird and thrush searching for the early worm ! How sweet the myriad honeysuckles in the green lanes, where the children already search for blackberries ! How pleasant the dinner at seven, with lights on the table, yet windows wide open to the lawn ! Assuredly I, with Horace, like my own *latebrae dulces* in September, and shall not easily be tempted away from them.

*   *   *   *   *

Earl Russell has recently taken occasion to remind us that he is the author of the terse definition of a proverb, 'The wisdom of many and the wit of one.' I am as great an admirer of proverbs as Sancho Panza and his younger brother, Sam Weller; and I think there is a good literary opening for anyone capable of collecting into a single essay the Wisdom of the Adage. Have none of the numerous bookmakers of the day wit enough to take the hint? Surely there were real epigrammatists among our proverb-making ancestors. Of how many modern poems may it not be said that they are 'Neither rhyme nor reason'? Do not Paternoster Row and Saville Row alike proclaim that 'Birds of a feather flock together'? Where is the man who has not in his time jumped 'Out of the frying-pan into the fire'? Who has ever attended a political or religious meeting without remembering that 'Speech is silvern, silence is golden'—an Arab proverb, by the way, and a great favourite of Mr. Carlyle's. Another quaint proverb of those descendants of the great Sheikh Ishmael who gave us algebra and almanacs, alembics and alkahests, is the following: 'To know the sea, live in it; to know the earth, sleep in it; to know the air, fly in it.' Captain Webb has, I suppose, made the closest approach to knowing the sea in this sense of any man on record:

> 'His fame has brought the adventurous Greeks to Lero, Hero would say, Leander is no hero.'

As to knowing the earth by sleeping in it, that we must all do in time. Whether, when the soft mould is mounded above us, the undying spirit will take note of its hitherto inseparable companion then decaying, is a question that has much exercised morbid speculators. I do not see that it matters much. If the free spirit is of a sentimental rather than an adventurous turn of mind, I can imagine its coming to stroll occasionally in the churchyard where its mortal remains were deposited. William Wordsworth would perhaps occasionally revisit the God's Acre of Grassmere; but David Livingstone would be anxious to explore Sirius or Aldebaran as soon as possible. In such circumstances we should verify the third clause of the Arab proverb, 'know the air.'

Sept. 9.

I am an optimist, and hate tragedies. For

Thoughts in my Garden. 213

once I read the 'Prometheus Bound' or 'Hamlet,' I read 'The Birds' or 'As You Like It' fifty times. The obvious reply is that life hath its tragedies, and that literature must be true to life. I do not quite agree herewith. I hold that the highest literature would deal with a life wherein tragedies are impossible. 'An imaginary life!' says the reader. True; but wherefore was imagination given unless we are to deal with scenes imaginary? Life without the Stock Exchange and the Army and Navy, without the police and the gallows, is surely a thing imaginable, if not attainable. And to it the function of poetry and romance should tend. Life as it should be is what I am prepared to welcome. Life as it ought not to be, and more hideous than it ever can become, is what we find depicted by most writers of fiction. I fancy the lady authors are fondest of these odious figments.

A lady writes to me: 'How I wish all the really jolly people in England would settle in one spot! The other parts of the country would be unspeakably dreary, but that wouldn't matter, and I dare say they [who? ladies' grammar] would be very content with their dulness.' I agree. The notion is a good one; why should it not be carried out on a grand scale? Let all the various people who go in for the same sort of thing be located (as the Yankees say) in the same neighbourhood. I imagine myself on a walking tour, with a pocket compass and a map of Oddshire to assist me. I arrive at cross-roads; a guide-post, thank Hermes. The right—Woman's Rights Village; the left—Flirtation Village. I put it to the most sedate young statesman of the day (Sir Wilfrid Lawson, let me say, or Sir Charles Dilke), would he turn right or left? I should prefer Flirtation Village myself, but then I am a Bohemian—*Rex Bohemiæ* before my abdication. Well, imagine another turning: right, Sir Wilfrid Lawson's toast and water: left—a perennial fountain of Allsopp and Bass. Which way, O wayfarer? I fear—I sadly fear—that the impulsive young student of Joe Miller would not have a triumphant majority of travellers. Toast and water may look pretty in a fountain, but weak humanity preferreth malt and hops ingeniously combined.

Sept. 16.

What influence can glue have upon literature? This looks like a conundrum, but is nothing of the sort. A publisher was having a friendly chat on my lawn the other day—for authors and publishers are not always enemies, though there are some publishers who justify Peter Pindar's famous saying that they drink their wine out of the skulls of authors. However, my friend and I were discussing why, though the incomes of almost all classes have gone up, those of authors (except in a few cases) are gradually diminishing. Many causes for this were mentioned, and among them one quite new to me—*videlicet*, glue. It seems that, for some mysterious reason, glue has recently risen from thirty to eighty pounds a ton; wherefore the bookbinders, to whom glue is a necessity, have raised their price. Now the binding is not the *chief* part of a book; and the Germans and French and Americans are so far ahead of us English, with all our boast of being the foremost nation in the world, that they issue books in paper covers, so that the purchaser need not pay for a binding unless he deems the book worth it, and can also bind it in the style which suits the subject and the writer. Well, the English bookbinder will have his price, or strike, and so will paper-makers and printers, and the public won't give more than a guinea or two a year to Mr. Mudie for its literature, heedless of Mr. Ruskin's statement that it is a sin to read a book unless you have bought it; and as it is only fair that publishers should live in pleasant mansions with deer parks, why, of course, it is the author who must suffer. He sets the mill going, but it does not grind for him. He may be as brilliant and instructive as he pleases, but he will never earn a competence, unless glue goes down. He may pine for a rump-steak, while the bookbinder eats his with oyster sauce.

* * * * *

I was over at Wargrave a few days ago in search of a friend who loves the Thames. I missed him, so I looked in at Mrs. Wyatt's and enjoyed a glass of something refrigerant. The new sign of the George and Dragon, painted by two A.R.A.'s who stay at Wargrave, is capital. St. George slaying the dragon is, as it ought to be, heroic; but the other side, St. George's draconic victim lying extinct, and St. George's horse looking gravely on, while St. George himself thirstily quaffs a tankard of bitter ale, is perfectly delightful. It makes one thirsty, which is, of course, exactly what an inn sign ought to do.

By the way, talking of thirst, I did rather a clever thing the other day. Sitting on the top of a coach, I remarked that it was impossible to brew good ale in Berkshire. I was unaware that the two leading brewers of the county were close to me, one just in front and the other at my side. I reached home in safety.

Sept. 23.

It is refreshing to find that there is at last a movement in favour of resuscitating the old style of female education. The inventor of the pianoforte has much to answer for. True, it was but a gradual development of the virginals and harpsichord, and Queen Elizabeth played the former instrument; but, had she been obliged to practise as many hours and days as a modern school-girl, she would never have been the accomplished woman she evidently was. Ladies like Mrs. Browning and Mrs. Webster show us what mastery of classic literature the female intellect can attain; while Mrs. Somerville alone proves that they can make immense progress in the infinite fields of mathesis. There are manifest reasons why only a small minority of women can become scholars or mathematicians in the highest sense; the chief being that most women marry, and that all women who wisely marry merge their individuality in that of their husband. I do not say they *lose* their original character: there is a change on both sides in a marriage of completion. Just as water, though made of oxygen and hydrogen, is neither the one nor the other, though containing both—just as salt is neither the gas chlorine nor the metal sodium—so people properly married become a duplex entity. When women do get a really good education, it will be curious to note the result where a mathematician weds a poetess, a botanist a Greek scholar, a novelist an architect, and so forth *ad infinitum*. I commend this new idea to our lady novelists, who seem terribly driven for fresh themes.

Sept. 30.

I had a schoolfellow, a very good fellow, with but one fault—he would argue. We christened him Syllogisticus. It was he who first introduced me to the famous though slightly dubious syllogism :

> 'Nothing is better than a virtuous life ;
> Bread and cheese is better than nothing ;
> *Ergo*—bread and cheese is better than a virtuous life.'

He also propounded that ancient dilemma concerning the king who built a bridge, and set up a gallows at the end of it, whereon he hanged anyone who, being questioned as to his object in crossing the bridge, told an untruth. At length there came a very logical traveller, who said, 'I am come to be hanged on that gallows.' Quoth the king to himself: 'If I hang that man he will have told the truth, and ought not to have been hanged. If I do not hang him he will have told a lie, and ought to have been hanged.' Perplexed by this insoluble problem, the king forthwith hanged himself.

Syllogisticus still lives, though his logical tendencies have given him a world of trouble through life. When he was a fag at school, he used to argue on the impropriety of his having to run after the balls at cricket practice; the logical reply was a tunding with a stump. He has been known to argue with the head-master as to whether he ought to be swished until fourteen cuts instead of seven were inflicted;

> 'To stripe the nether urchin like a pink
> Or tender hyacinth, inscribed with woe,'

as Tom Hood poetically puts it. When he took to the life of London, he was admittedly the most dexterous disputant in Bohemia; and his tendency has stood him in good stead, for no man living has written more brilliant leaders, taking every possible side of every possible question. He regards religion and politics and literature with a lofty impartiality. He has written Evangelical tracts, and strong articles for a Roman Catholic journal. The way in which he has shown Gladstone to be a nobody is only surpassed by the style in which he has shown Disraeli to be a wind-bag. 'What am I to prove?' he says to his editor. 'Tell me that, and the thing is done. A logician can prove anything.' Need I say that the able pen of Syllogisticus is in immense demand?

He has just been pitching into me for my remarks on Mr. Newdegate's speech last week. We had been dining quietly at the Chandos Club—the only club in London where you meet men who know a thing or two. Talk has so degenerated into gossip that clubs have become a nuisance, and oh! how offensive is the fellow who talks you a *Times* leader on the Herzegovina which you found too dull to read, or gives as great news one of the *Athenæum's* important facts about the forthcoming work of small novelists and smaller poets. The man who invents scandal about his neighbours' wives is more amusing. Well, Syllogisticus, having glanced through last week's notes somewhat contemptuously, drinks a glass of Lafitte, and opens on me thus :

No happiness but in labour! That's Mr. Newdegate's thesis—and not his alone, but that of men like Lord Derby, who prefers a Bluebook to his father's 'Iliad.' I say that the most perfect happiness is not work, but play. And I also say that men like Mr. Newdegate don't know the meaning of work. They are doing what they like : that I call play, not work. No man knows what work means unless he lives by it. If I dropped my quill, sir, I should get no dinner : the gentlemen who lecture on labour, and whose dinner is safe, cannot understand that. They can stop when they are tired ; I have had to work till my brain would move no longer, and I sank on my bed insensible, with a terrible illness before me. That's work, if you will. *Laborare est orare,* said the old monks. *Laborare est vitâ frui,* say the modern lecturers. Both true, within limits. My labour is prayer now, because I am teaching men and women what they would not have learnt without my aid. My labour is life-enjoyment now, because I am not working in absolute dread of starvation, which has been my lot. But I repeat that the man born to affluence, whatever he achieves by volunteer industry, never works at all. He does good, doubtless; he can be no more said to work than a polo-player, or Grace on the cricket-field, or Dr. Pusey when he sits down to chess with a competent opponent. It is only play. The test of *work* is—Do you live by it? Unless you do, I defy you to understand the real feelings of a working-man. I hate work. I specially hate the only kind of work that I find pays; but one must live, you know. . . . Waiter, another bottle of that Lafitte.

* * * * *

What odd things happen! Who will rebel next? The silly season has had its excitements, and now we hear that those hitherto well-behaved insects, the bees, are in a state of mutiny! What would Virgil say? He writes (I quote my friend Mr. Blackmore's version):

> 'The sage affirms that bees (a favoured line)
> Participate intelligence divine,
> And draughts ethereal from the fountain-head.
> For God pervadeth all, above, around,
> The earth, the ocean, and the heaven profound.
> From Him the flocks, the herds, mankind, and brutes,
> Each one at birth his subtle life recruits;
> To Him again doth all creation yearn,
> And solved into its elements return;
> No room for death—all quick with life they fly
> Unto the roll of stars and heritage of sky.'

Well, the bees this year are eating wall-fruit ferociously, and stinging with unusual sharpness of acupuncture. I was of opinion that this was due to scarcity of honey, as the honey-yielding flowers have been drenched by incessant rains; but Mr. Clegram, a beekeeper of forty years' standing, who feeds his bees at the hives, states that they have spoilt his peaches and nectarines for some years past. He thinks that, perhaps, in the general progress of things, even the bees may be growing demoralised, and taking to short hours and less labour. So high an authority should not be carelessly questioned; but I think that, in default of flowers, the bees will prefer fruit to sugar administered at the hives. How would it be for fruit-growers to plant thyme, melilot, melianthus, and mignonette near their southern walls? The most fertile of the common flowers just now is the Michaelmas daisy—a species of aster; and on a clump of these in a cottage garden I have just seen myriads of bees, and a great number of butterflies. As this flower comes just when peaches are ripening, might not fruit-growers use it to advantage?

Oct. 7.

I had a long letter the other day from a peer of the realm—five sheets of Bath post—in reference and partial reply to an article of mine. Now, with all the desire in the world to be courteous, I fear I shall not succeed, for my correspondent's writing is such that I cannot make out more than a third of his communication. I do him no harm by mentioning this fact: doubtless the printers who have had to set up his MSS. would thank me if I could induce him to write in clearer form. Why should men write badly for the fun of it? 'Punctuality is the politeness of princes,' is a maxim that has been attributed to a King of France and also to a King of England. A kindred aphorism might be that a clear hand-writing is the courtesy of gentlemen. Ladies may do as they like: but I must say I prefer their letters when legible.

* * * * *

The photographic art is really a great delight, although it is mathematically impossible that a photograph can be accurate. This notion occurred to me when, suddenly looking up, I saw several portraits of people I greatly admire, and also of people I wholly despise. I think it satisfactory to have both in front of you. A man can't get through life without many troubles; but, if courageous and adventurous, he will also have plenty of enjoyment. Life is what man makes it. If I see in my picture gallery an abominable creature, I also see some one brighter and truer than any heroine of Shakespeare's. Life has its rewards, and the beauty and wisdom of womanhood are too great to be put in prose. Poetry is not permitted here.

* * * * *

Having written leading articles for about thirty years, I know their absurdity in daily papers; it is absolutely impossible for the quickest political journalist to make up his mind on a question with no information but a few hasty and inaccurate telegrams. However, the public must have leaders, as they like to be led. They want to be able to talk politics. Often, in a railway carriage, I have had a fellow talk to me the article I had written a few hours before, after hearing a debate in the House. I, of course, contradict such people on every point, just for the fun of it.

Oct. 14.

I want to know why women cannot whistle? They claim to be able to do anything that a man can do—of course I speak of the strong-minded section of "the frail sect." They can talk and write—that's clear—and I dare say they think they can fight, though probably they would not have courage enough to cut off their left breasts like the Amazons, just to make fighting easy. But why can't they whistle? 'A whistling wife is like a crowing hen,' says a Scottish proverb. When I was a boy it used to be thought great fun to chaff the girls about their whistling incapacity. I confess I wish that boys could not whistle, for the cacophonous row they make is abominable; but there is no Act of Parliament to put it down, and they will do it.

* * * * *

This is just the time for walnuts with your port, and there are scarcely any good walnuts. The reason of this I am about to mention, hoping the erudite S. H., pleasantly oracular on all such topics, will not incontinently prove me wrong.* People *pick* walnuts nowaday. In my boyhood they went up the trees and thrashed them down with long sticks. The

---

* Mr. Shirley Hibberd had found fault with some previous remark.

walnut tree, like the small boy, improves with a 'tunding.'

> 'A spaniel, a woman, a walnut tree,
> The more you beat 'em, the better they be.'

I have never had the opinion of a committee of ladies or of spaniels on this old couplet, but I believe it to be quite true of what in my youth in the west country we called the welshnut tree.

*　　*　　*　　*　　*

In a clever story in the *World*, called 'Lady Raby's Misfortunes,' Mr. John Dangerfield maintains that an ugly man cannot be a great orator. He thinks that such a man can terrify, but not persuade. How about Mirabeau? If that man had lived, there would have been no French revolution. He had the power of conciliating both the Court and the nation. Yet was there ever uglier man? Or Jack Wilkes—who boasted that, ugly as he was, he would beat any man in love-making with half an hour's start? Or Brougham, who talked Greek fire, and whose queer little nose could not remain still for an instant on his parchment face?

* * * * *

The question has arisen, in connexion with a story recently published, whether it is proper to sketch a little girl climbing a tree. We are a very virtuous nation, and the idea of a female child climbing a cedar at the age of fourteen seemed to a distinguished editor most indecorous. I ventured to object to his views, and asked a few ladies their opinion on the subject. They had all, though of patrician birth, climbed trees in their girlhood: one said the happiest hours of her life were passed in a tree—another that she was quite willing to climb any tree on my lawn at that moment. Still I am not satisfied. Perchance these ladies were Bohemians in early youth. Will any lady-reader of the primmest propriety, who has read Hannah More and Mrs. Trimmer and Mrs. Markham and Miss Mangnall, kindly tell me if she climbed a tree when she wore short frocks, and whether she was found out and punished by her austere governess? I really want to know. I have helped so many merry children to climb trees that, if the distinguished editor is right, I have a deep burden of iniquity upon me.*

* The novel in question was the author's 'Sweet and Twenty,' of which a review had been written for the *Times*, which the late Mr. Delane, then editor, declined to insert, because he found that the heroine of the book climbed trees. Mortimer Collins's appeal to his lady readers of prim proprieties resulted in his being very cleverly hoaxed by one of his female friends, a lively and witty lady, who sent him a letter which seems worth quoting.

'Kensington, October.

'Sir,—As one who has gone through a course of Hannah More, Mrs. Trimmer, and Mangnall's Questions, I venture to give my opinion on the subject of girls climbing trees, as requested in your "Adversaria," of October 15th. Pardon me, if, as an old woman of the old school, I take a wrong view of the case, for in this age it is necessary that the old should ask the pardon of those younger, and, therefore, better informed than themselves. As one of the middle-class, who, I have noticed, think far more of the proprieties of life (pruderies, perhaps, you would call them) than either the patrician or the peasant, my opinion may have some weight.

' In my young days I read Mrs. Trimmer's histories, seated decorously in my proper place in class (never, I regret to say, a very high one) at the day-school in Islington, which I regularly attended; Hannah More and Mangnall's Questions being lessons that were learnt by heart at home, and repeated at school, were almost invariably studied, when the weather permitted, up in the boughs of a large old apple-tree in the

Oct. 21.

The dulness of the present autumn is really portentous. As I write I look out on a lime-orchard that lay at the back of the old-fashioned flower garden, both belonging to the house my father rented. There were gardens and orchards in those days at Islington. Alas! ugly rows of brick houses with back-yards now occupy the spot where I have spent so many happy hours. But, sir, I fear it was owing to that very apple tree that I won no prizes at school, that I was never first in my class, nor ever in the first class. Who could properly study Mangnall or Hannah More by heart while a thousand delightful distractions were passing under one's eyes? Can I ever forget the scent of the flowers wafted from the neighbouring gardens; the fresh grass of the orchard pied with field flowers, the bees that hummed drowsily around, the insects that darted to and fro, the birds that flitted from tree to tree, and that I grew to look upon as friends? Could I read when the robin lighted on one of the very boughs of the tree in which I was perched, while I held my breath in delighted terror lest the moving of a leaf should scare him? Could I trouble my head with questions of historic worthies who lived and died so many years ago, when I discovered the nest, with four young sparrows, in the laurel hedge close by me?

'When I grew tired of rural delights I could climb still higher, and from the topmost bough catch a glimpse of a busy thoroughfare, with shops and a constant succession of carriages and horses and foot-passengers—a panorama of ever-varied and never-ending delight.

'Then that day when a pig escaped from its drover, and ran down the back lane that divided our orchard from the neighbouring garden, and declined, on any terms, to return the way it was required. The pleasure of the spectacle was

Thoughts in my Garden.

shaded lawn, washed by the ever-descending deluge. It is pretty, but very chilly. The limes are tinged with yellow; a copper beech

enhanced, because I had a companion that day to share it.

'With what thrilling interest we watched the struggle from the apple-boughs, and how we sympathised with the pig. How we cheered when by a sudden turn he evaded the enemy and ran grunting down the lane! How we wished there might be *one* weak spot in our well-kept palings by which he might have escaped into our orchard, whence nothing should have induced us to give him up again to his owner. History could scarcely offer an instance of greater treachery! When, at last, after a desperate resistance, he was recaptured and ignominiously driven back by a string tied to his leg, how we hoped that he might yet once more effect his escape, and pictured him wandering, free and unpursued, in the green lanes of Hornsey. But the next day at school I remember well that I was taken down six places, and had a task to learn that kept me hours in class afterwards.

'So, sir, I think I must give my opinion against the practice of girls climbing trees. To this I attribute much of my ignorance on subjects which it was my duty to learn. 'Tis true that I grew straight and supple as an ash sapling, while my cousins, who went to a neighbouring boarding-school (where they learnt everything that was thought necessary to one's education in those days), though they suffered hours of agony with the back-board and the stocks, yet complained all their lives of weakness of the spine, and could never walk a mile without tiring. Still they could set me right on a thousand things of which I was ignorant, just as now my youngest grandson finds numberless occasions of correcting me, or giving me information, in a doubtless well-

burns opposite with colours indescribable; blackbirds and song-thrushes and missel-thrushes are making fine meals upon worms, and talking to each other musically. But the water is running down the paths, and I fear all the flavour will be washed out of my medlars. This is distinctly weather in which one must make one's own sunshine. Happy the man who has a loving wife and faithful friends—the best materials for that manufacture.

And, dear reader, who hast faithfully accom-

---

intended spirit, but for which in my young days he would have suffered soundly in the flesh. Apologising for this long and I fear tedious letter (but the old are ever garrulous on the subject of their youth),

'I remain, sir, yours respectfully,
'ONE OF THE OLD SCHOOL.'

The writer of this was a young lady, a most intimate friend of Mortimer Collins's; but he was quite taken in with it, and made the following comment:

'The exquisite poetic irony of this letter needs no comment from me. I thank its author heartily. Straight and supple as an ash sapling in her girlhood, I know that she is wise and noble in her grandmotherhood: and, had I the honour and pleasure of her acquaintance, I should certainly treat her with more deference than that forward "youngest grandson," to whom a little suffering in the flesh would be of use.'—F. C.

panied me through long columns of 'Adversaria'*
for many a long year, dost thou not find that
this pluvious weather produceth much newspaper stupidity? The duller the weather the
duller the writer. Nothing happens. Thiers
has been talking about nothing particular.
There have been meetings and congresses.
Why the deuce (pardon the slip, O editor!)
cannot people hold congresses in their own
parlours, and settle matters in a quieter, wiser
way? About the Social Science Congress I
care nothing; it is simply an arrangement
whereby unscientific people talk what they
fancy is science. It is below contempt, and
excellently adapted to the effervescent ab-
surdities of Brighton. But a Church Congress
I regard as an offence against the Church of
England. I deem that Church a great power
in the world—for if not so it is a mere sham—
and I hold that its subaltern officers should
obey their superiors; holding also that archbishops and bishops should obey the law of
the Church. It seems to me (under correction)

* The chief part of these papers were entitled 'Adversaria.'

that the great axiom that those who desire to command must first learn to obey is altogether disregarded. But that axiom is true; command without previous obedience is impossible.

Dean Hook is dead: nephew of Theodore Hook, and an able man in his way. I don't care about a man who thinks it necessary to be a teetotaler, and I think his Archiepiscopal Lives rather weak and thin. I have a hatred of extremes. It seems to me rather weak that the Vicar of Leeds (himself not a drunkard, yet enjoying his glass of wine) should give sanction to the restraint of drunkards by joining them in a vow of abstinence. What pleasure would there have been in offering the Dean a glass of sound old port? And will anyone dare to tell me a Dean is any the worse for liking his glass of sound old port?

I am not writing ironically or sardonically. I hold that a Churchman in holy orders should be, above all things, human. Some of our young parsons put on divinity as if it were a fashionable overcoat. But humanity is the first thing, and divinity may well come second. It is easier to understand man or woman than to understand the Creator of men and women. These young theologic adepts fancy they know everything: the blunders they consequently make are awful.

Hurrah! The sun has actually burst through the lime-trees. I shall cut my notes short (at risk of angering my courteous editor) and rush away into the upper country. *Vale.*

Oct. 23.

Two friends, whom I will call the Antiquary and the Wanderer, came to see me on Saturday last, and greatly interfered with my literary work. Forgive me, apprehensive reader; if sometimes I did not receive stray visitors I should not give you half the number of ideas that now bubble up in this column. There were days when I was a Londoner as well as a 'Loiterer.' I know my London now as well as any man living, but I prefer the country. What I like is to get my London friends to visit me, and bring the airy rumours of the town, the latest wit and wisdom of the clubs.

It is very charming, over a wood fire, with a good cigar, to listen to the newest news and wittiest wit.

The Antiquary and the Wanderer, who had not met before, and whose ages differed by a year or two, got on together excellent well. As to the Antiquary, he and I never met without a friendly fight on politics.

My friend the Wanderer has been tramping through Hampshire and Wiltshire. I like a tramp of that kind, but am too busy to attempt it, and my numerous admirers have not yet offered me a two-horse omnibus to give me an autumnal tour. I have walked through most of England's counties, and written descriptions of many of my walks. The adventures you meet are delightful. Mr. Cook may take his people to the Nile and the Pyramids, as he at present advertiseth. But do those travellers know the Dart, or Wye, or Severn? Have they seen Stonehenge? The Wanderer was very savage about Stonehenge. He went there to enjoy a look at the grand old mysterious monument, and behold, Joseph Arch was there, holding a mutinous meeting. So a wayfarer who desired to study in quiet a marvellous monument of the past, was foiled by a 'fool with a circumbendibus,' as Coleridge has it, who was talking frightful nonsense to a lot of working men. If this Arch is to emit platitudes, surely he might choose some place fitter than the noblest and most mysterious of those ancient monuments which Parliament finds it so difficult to protect.

I get an immense quantity of 'loitering' correspondence, and am much obliged to my correspondents; but it is quite impossible to answer them all. A 'good few,' to use a country phrase, are poets; to them I should say, don't write a line until you have thoroughly mastered Shakespeare, Milton, and Byron. When you have done that, send a specimen of your verse to the 'Loiterer,' and he will (if he lives to the date of that thorough mastery) give you his unbiassed opinion, and (if the publishers of poetry still exist) recommend you to a publisher. But somebody said to somebody else, late at night, in the smoking-room of the Chandos Club, another man having just passed out, 'Poet, isn't he?' 'Yes.' 'Awful fool!' 'You're right.' 'Ever known a bigger fool?' 'Yes; man who publishes for him!'

Oct. 23.

A dear friend of mine, who knows I love old books if they are worth anything, has just given me a copy of Martial, published at Zurich in 1544, and bound in oak, with clasps. It is in a delightful Italic type. There's a treasure for you, O bibliophilist! The oak binding is a perfect piece of art, tooled with the care of those ancient days. The book itself is curious, being a rearranged edition. Martial, as all men know who have lived a part of their life in the Rome of Domitian and Trajan, brought out his volumes of epigrams successively. Altogether there were fifteen, counting the 'Spectaculorum Liber.' Conrad Gesner, of Zurich, begins on his title-page by remarking that all improprieties will be purged from the book, as it is intended for schools to use; then, instead of publishing

Martial as the greatest of all epigrammatists chose to publish himself, he classifies the epigrams according to their subjects. There are eighty-five divisions. Martial went over the same ground pretty often; but he was the mirror of Imperial Rome, and his record of that age is most valuable to all who study history. Few men know Martial thoroughly, he is so various. He was, in my judgment, a good fellow and a great satirist. To satirise the Rome of Domitian he was compelled to write what, of course, is unfit for boys and girls to read.

I transcribe the Horatian lines which the giver of that unique Martial put on the fly-leaf.[*] They flatter me, but they are too good to omit:

> ' Cæcilius! take this tome as tribute true,
> 'Tis rendering unto Cæsar Cæsar's due;
> For, if the best books should be his who best
> Can use them, this should surely bear your crest.
> To you its mighty strains—to me all mute—
> Are musical as is Apollo's lute!

---

[*] The poetic giver was Mr. Campkin, librarian of the Reform Club, and the 'Antiquary' mentioned in the former paragraph.—F. C.

> Since Zurich's press sent this brave volume forth,
> Three hundred years and thirty Mother Earth
> Hath added to her tale : while centuries
> Eighteen have lapsed since Martial oped his eyes,
> And, with his scorpion thong, essayed to lash
> The vices, follies, of his age. No flash
> Of summer lightning his stern verse illumes,
> But with Olympian bolts he smites, consumes.
> Thus he whose lightest line's a thunder-stroke
> Fit armour finds in panoply of oak.'

And a grand old panoply of oak it is ; and I ask you, gentle reader, Could friendly verse be more charming, more enjoyable ?

Curious that the Balaclava charge and the battle of Agincourt happened on the same day, and that nobody except *Notes and Queries* seemed to remember it. Now it is pretty well understood that the Balaclava charge was a mistake ; it showed glorious gallantry, but it was a blunder. And a far greater blunder was to allow capital to be made out of it at the Alexandra Palace. That was degrading, and the less said of it the better. The English soldier may be going downhill, but he has not yet reached the low level of the directors of public companies. I hold that the Balaclava charge, brilliant and brief, was a serious error. Our generals had not learnt the lesson of the time, and were unaware that the great winner of battles must always be heavy artillery, until some chemist discovers the deadly destructive of the future.

War, in fact, is becoming contemptible, and ought to be put down by the great nations of Europe, just as we put down a vulgar riot. Agincourt was as much greater than Balaclava as Drayton than Tennyson. King Harry knew what he meant to do, and he did it. The poetry of the day is really too ridiculous:

> Cannon to right of them,
> Cannon to left of them,
> Cannon behind them,
>   Volleyed and thundered.
>
> Stormed at with shot and shell,
> (Line that does very well,)
> Each fellow looks a swell,
> Means to use sabre well,
> Russians with steel to fell,
>   That's your Six Hundred.

I quote the Poet Laureate from memory: I have never forgiven him for rhyming *hundred* with *thundered*. A French lady asked an

Englishman what a false quantity meant; he said it was as bad in a man as a *faux pas* in a woman. What shall we say of the Poet Laureate's Cockney rhyme of 'hundred' with 'thundered'?

Now to take old Drayton on Agincourt, a battle which deserves its anniversary, for it was a great fight and a most noble victory. Do you see where Tennyson gets metre and thought? Here is Drayton's King Harry:

> 'And turning to his men,
>   Quoth our brave Henry then,
> "Though they be one to ten,
>   Be not amazed.
> Yet have we well begun,
> Battles so bravely won
> Have ever to the sun
>   By fame been raised.
>
> '"And for myself," quoth he,
> "This my full rest shall be:
> England ne'er mourn for me,
>   Nor more esteem me,
> Victor I will remain,
> Or on this earth be slain;
> Never shall she sustain
>   Loss to redeem me."'

He meant it, and he won that battle, with an overwhelming force against him. Here is the final stanza of the ballad by Drayton, on which Tennyson founded his much inferior sheaf:

> 'Upon St. Crispin's day,
> Fought was this noble fray ;
> Which fame did not delay
> To England to carry ;
> Oh! when shall English men
> With such acts fill a pen,
> Or England breed again
> Such a King Harry?'

Those two lines at the last are tremendously suggestive.

Nov. 4.

Old-fashioned autumns of serene calm and divine colour, old-fashioned frosty winters, seem to have disappeared. When I was ten years old the weather was very different from what we are treated with now. I was in Chatham in the year 1837, and well remember that the coach from the King's Head at Rochester could not, even with six horses, force its way toward Canterbury. I was rather a loiterer in those days, though a small boy in short frocks, and liable to occasional whippings. But I looked at the world, even as a bather looks on the sea when the mornings are chilly; and I thought to myself 'twas a cold world into which to plunge. Yet, having made my plunge, I do not even now find it terribly cold. There is a little warmth here and there.

Anything like the cold at Chatham in that year 1837 I do not remember. The very tea froze in the teapot. The sentinels at Tom All Alone and the Fire Barn on Chatham Lines were almost frozen to death. Sheep by thousands were lost in the snow. And then there was such wind. I remember an elderly lady, umbrella and pattens and all, being caught up by a wind-eddy, and carried many feet above her natural level. She fortunately descended safely enough. Now I wonder whether it is all the effusion of railway steam that turns snow into rain. Is it the vapour of a million trains which is coming down upon us in this unpleasant fashion?

* * * * *

Will the present mania for theology and science come to an end? Will pure English literature, the greatest of all educating powers, get another chance? I say nothing against true religion; but shallow brains are driven wild by polemic theology. I say nothing against thoughtful science; but I protest against claptrap lectures with showy experiments, which teach nothing. What with Vatican pamphlets, and pseudo-science, and the foolish modern novels that appear at the rate of five a week on an average, real literature gets no chance. There are plenty of periodicals, you may say, and they contain wonderfully clever things. True, but how much is spontaneity, how much mere manufacture? Even as the Royal Academy has a tendency to kill high art, so has the modern periodical to kill pure letters. An author must live, and he generally does live, and gets his occasional rump steak, though of course he leaves the oyster sauce to the more generous table of his publisher. But, unless he is lucky enough to begin life with no need for work, he will almost surely be driven to do work which he despises. The harm of this is great, but there is no remedy, unless the people could be educated, and the school boards are not going the right way to do that. Education for adults is now in the hands of the Press, and the Press declines to do it. It gives enormous space to sensational topics, and no room to what is of real importance.

※　　※　　※　　※　　※

Two young ladies, great friends of mine, lived some years ago at Winchester. Of course they were great believers in the pluck and prowess of Winchester schoolboys. Well, a cricket match came off between Eton and England's ancient capital : and very close the young gentlemen ran each other. When they went to lunch, things were so evenly balanced that the excitement was enormous : the girls ran home for their lunch also, and found (oh, rapture !) a box containing new silk dresses from their London dressmaker. If my little friend Clara, who told me the story, were not as perfect as a pearl (which, by the way, *does* rhyme with girl) I could not have believed the sequel. They did not open the box which contained those delights and vanities in which they were to adorn their pretty persons, but rushed back to see the rest of the match! Alas, Winchester was beaten by one run. But it was afterwards acknowledged that either scorer or umpire had made a blunder, and that virtually the match was a draw.

Another story of a Winchester boy from the same source amused me. The *pia mater* of my friends is slightly democratic, has in a conservatory a vine from Garibaldi's stock, whose grapes she sends to her friends as of immense value, and corresponds with Mr. Disraeli's character in 'Lothair,' the charming Mrs. Putney Giles. Well, this Winchester youngster was, under the influence of cake and wine, discoursing to her concerning the misery of fagging and the anguish of being 'tunded.' The commiserative old lady filled his glass with more sherry, and suggested that when he got into the higher form he should not fag or 'tund' anybody.

'Oh, won't I!' said he.

Nov. 18.

Here is a poetic picture of the modern Baiæ, written in 1868:

> Will there be snowfall on lofty Soracte
>   After a summer so tranquil and torrid?
> Whoso detests the East wind, as a fact he
>   Thinks 'twill be horrid.
> But there are zephyrs more mild by the ocean,
>   Every keen touch of the snowdrifts to lighten:
> If to be cosy and snug you've a notion—
>   Winter at Brighton!
>
> Politics nobody cares about. Spurn a
>   Topic whereby all our happiness suffers.
> Dolts in the back streets of Brighton return a
>   Couple of duffers.
> Fawcett and White in the Westminster Hades,
>   Strive the reporters' misfortunes to heighten.
> What does it matter? Delicious young ladies
>   Winter in Brighton.
>
> Good is the turtle for luncheon at Mutton's.
>   Good is the hock that they give you at Bacon's
> Mainwaring's fruit in the bosoms of gluttons
>   Yearning awakens.
> Buckstone comes hither, delighting the million,
>   'Mid the theatrical minnows a Triton;
> Dickens and Lemon pervade the Pavilion—
>   Winter at Brighton!
>
> If you've a thousand a-year, or a minute—
>   If you're a D'Orsay, whom everyone follows;
> If you've a head—'tis no matter what's in it—
>   Fair as Apollo's;

Thoughts in my Garden. 251

If you approve of flirtations; good dinners:
Seacapes divine which the merry winds whiten—
Nice little saints, and still nicer young sinners—
Winter in Brighton!

Alack and alas! only seven years ago, and we have lost Charles Dickens and Mark Lemon. Buckstone still lives, a noble evergreen. All three were at Brighton that winter, if I remember aright. Mutton, of course, is immortal so near the South Downs. Mainwaring, the fruiterer, has vanished from the scene. Has he taken with him his tame blackbird, Jack? He was taken out of a nest in a churchyard wall, unfledged; and when I first knew him he was a splendid fellow. He inhabited the shop, pecked at the fruit, kept down the spiders. To see him fly at the caterpillars when they were unpacking cabbages in the morning was delightful. He flew quite trustfully into your hand, and was wont to follow Mr. Mainwaring through the crowded traffic of the King's Road. Once I saved his life. The shop had been painted. He got some paint on his claws, and pecked it off. When I went in for my morning figs, everybody was in sore distress. Poor Jack was lying senseless on a patch of grass, apparently at the last gasp. I got some castor-oil and a quill, and dosed the poor bird. In ten minutes he was able to walk about. The fact is, perchance, worth recording in case anybody should have a pet bird in similar condition. But I wonder what has become of poor dear Jack, whose friendly pecks I shall never feel again.

Dec. 9.

Looking through the *Berkshire Chronicle*, I came upon a meeting of Good Templars. I was sorry to see a clergyman stating that, ' if he had to live his life over again he should devote it to the temperance cause.' Surely a clergyman who says this must be utterly blind to the importance of his office. Does not the gospel of Christ, which it is his happy prerogative to teach and to illustrate by his daily life, *include* temperance? Does he really think that a teetotal lecturer can do more good than a priest of the Church of England? Does he wholly forget that the first miracle recorded

Thoughts in my Garden. 253

of our Lord was changing water into wine at a bridal feast.

The question between men of sense and Good Templars divides itself into two parts—moral and physical. As to the physical point, observe this: there are some men of a gross type or an excitable type, apoplectic or fidgety, to whom a glass of wine is poison. It makes one class stupid, driving the blood to the head; it maddens the other. It is well that such persons should be Good Templars. But is the man who can drink wine wisely to cut himself down to the weak pattern of these morbid muffs? Perish the thought! Did not Noah plant the vine, my clerical friend? Did not Christ drink wine at that great Supper which we celebrate? Christianity means a sensible and reasonable life, a complete development of humanity; to fetter it with teetotal or any similar rules is to forget that freedom is its very essence. Christ left the deeds of men to their conscience, which is God speaking to the soul.

Dec. 16.

What are the sanitary inspectors about? What, to venture a step farther, are country gentlemen about, in some parts of this highly civilised England? I hear to-day of a cottage, with two bedrooms only, inhabited by a labouring man and his wife, two daughters, one married and the other not, the married one's husband and infant, and four children of the old man's son, who is a gentleman's coachman in London. The old man is in bed with typhoid fever; his wife, weakened by chronic asthma, died on Tuesday night last, and will not be buried till Sunday. The four young grandchildren sleep in the same room with the old man; the two daughters and son-in-law and a baby are in the other room—with the dead body. This is stern fact. The rooms are not much more than cupboards. There are several clergy close by, and one has just announced a Penny Reading for Monday next. Could he not read Tom Hood's 'Lay of the Labourer'? However, it may be no duty of the progressive parsons and rich squires of the neighbourhood to help their poorer neighbours; but it must surely be the duty of the Inspector of Nuisances to invite the magistrates to condemn such a cottage as that which I have described. Everyone who has inquired into the way in which the poor are often compelled to live must have been horrified at arrangements which make filth, disease, and incest inevitable. Parish doctors are so over-worked that they have no time to keep up with modern medical science. The squire's wife sends to London for a medical baronet, when requiring medical aid. Opposite the squire's gate there are a row of cottages where the inmates are crowded like rabbits in a warren, and which are a real fever-factory. I am not writing from imagination.* I believe in country gentlemen as a great English institution, if they do their duty in the old sound way. But there are too many *parvenu*

* This was in the neighbourhood of Mortimer Collins's cottage at Knowl Hill. He gave great offence by his courageous exposure, on more than one occasion, of the wretched state of the cottages of the poor.—F. C.

squireens nowaday, *novi homines*, with no real old root in the soil. It is a time

' When wealth accumulates, and men decay.'

*   *   *   *   *

Dear reader, have you ever written a poem whose sublimity makes the publishers shudder? If so, you will sympathise with me. I have a poem in manuscript of about the length of the *Iliad*, which has almost caused two or three publishers' readers to commit suicide.* I am going to inflict on you, in this connection, two stanzas of it :

> Helen and I look out upon the West,
> O unimaginable sunset! O
> Soft sky in mystic waves of colour drest,
> With great Apollo's final kiss aglow!
> O lights that lessen, linger, glisten, grow!
> Almighty Artist, never do I see
> Thy little, lightest touch of fire or snow,
> Of bird that sings, of blossom upon tree
> Without this inner silent saying : *I love Thee.*

---

* This poem remains unpublished.— F. C.

Some men defy Thee, some deny Thee ; ay,
And there are some who fear Thee. Wherefore so ?
As I look up to Thy great arch of sky,
As I look round where all Thy roses grow,
Can I defy, deny, or fear ? *O no!*
Best friend of mine art Thou ; father and friend.
Thy very voice and touch I think I know,
And half believe that Thou dost condescend
To tell me truths unheard. I trust Thee to the end.

CHAPTER VII.

1876.

Ah, the most ancient time,
   When God and man were friends,
And earth was rounded with a summer clime,
   And the dull doubt that lends
Sorrow to life was all a thing unknown.
   Before those hours had flown
God walked at eventide thro' Eden's shade
And spoke to man, and man was not afraid.

Cannot that time return?
   Is it not here for those
Who from the strong still work of God can learn
   His grandeur of repose?
A day with Him is as a myriad years,
   A tear outweighs the spheres;
And as He walked 'neath Eden's mystic tree,
In the cool eventide He walks with me.

Jan. 1.

A well-known writer is good enough to thank me for certain points in my Loiterings, and I hereby reciprocate his appreciation. As a fact, the commonwealth of letters would be a great power in England if men of letters were less jealous and more ready to be *bon camarade*. So, when a strange hand is held out to grasp mine, faith, I like it. We are all working together: if we don't quite agree with each other's ways of work, the end is clear. What do we want? The poetry of life. We leave its prose to millionaires.*

Jan. 6.

Rats are prolific. I bought two white rats on the first Saturday in August, 1875, and by the end of December they had increased to forty-nine. The increase would have been greater had I not committed a series of infanticides, and given three litters, in all thirty-two, to some tame owls, who evidently found

---

* I have referred to M. C.'s geniality and the warmth of his friendship, when once established, in the little prefatory sketch to these volumes.—E. Y.

them very nice for breakfast. I now believe the story of the 'Pied Piper of Hamelin,' which Robert Browning has turned into such delightful doggrel. If rats do get the upper hand, they must be something tremendous. I wish the painter of that capital picture, 'A Fascinating Tail,' could see my sixteen white rats (three generations of them) frolicking about in a large cage, and emitting occasional squeaks, while a Skye terrier (as quick a ratter as ever breathed) sits on his haunches and looks at them with melancholy eyes. He knows he must not touch one even if it should squeeze through the bars of the cage, which now and then happens, since they eat away the woodwork; but I think Master Rory, who is called Dolls for short, believes I am keeping those rats for a grand field-day, when he will have his innings. The fur of these white rats, when clean, is very soft and beautiful; I should think it would be quite possible for furriers to make good use of it for the decoration of ladies' mantles; and, as they multiply so rapidly and give no trouble, the notion seems worth a thought, seeing that we hunt ermine and sable at a vast expenditure.

* * * * *

A gentleman of high standing and rare accomplishments remarked, in conversation some time ago, that 'literary men are best at a distance.' I believe he is fond of a paradox. At the same time he may have had reason for what he said. There *are* literary men who contrive to make themselves offensive in general society. There is the man of real genius, never thoroughly accepted by the public, who revenges himself by caustic epigram at the dinner-table. There is the man to whom anything which can be caricatured is irresistible, and who puts all his acquaintances into novels with the slight disguise of names, a practice which cannot be too severely reprobated. There is the man who cannot tolerate average folly, and comes down with sledge-hammer force upon anyone who talks nonsense. There is the youthful poetaster who likes to recite his love-lyrics to young ladies, when they would far prefer some gayer amusement with some less conceited young gentleman. In ordinary society, I concede that all these people, and more that I could indicate, are intolerable bores. Perhaps the *Ursus Maximus* of letters was dear old Samuel Johnson, yet had no man heartier friends, and he was well beloved by Sir Joshua Reynolds, the most courteous and elegant of men. Genius has its drawbacks. It is believed that Shakespeare occasionally drank too much; it is certain that Pope libelled ladies and played ungentlemanly tricks. One would rather have the faults—not to mention the genius—of William Shakespeare than of Alexander Pope. However, the fact is that the Man of Letters can only be understood by the most highly civilised society, such as that of Athens in the days of Pericles, by Rome in those of Augustus. I suppose neither Mr. Gladstone nor Mr. Disraeli would maintain that he is the equal of Mæcenas, and it is certain that no King of England since Henry VIII. has been equal to Augustus Cæsar. But look at Horace's familiar verses to the Minister! look at Virgil's easy letters to the Emperor! Mæcenas wrote uncommonly bad verse, and would probably have translated Homer as weakly as Mr. Gladstone; but he knew good poetry when he saw it, and he knew how to reward and encourage a poet. If Horace had lived in England he would have had a paltry pension of fifty pounds, instead of a country estate on which he could live as a gentleman, without a care, and devote his power to the benefit of Rome.

Jan. 13.

'The mesmeriser snow.' Charming phrase, that of Browning's. Snow is mesmerising us at this moment—casting a strange, sleepy feeling over the world. The east wind drives the sharp white shower along the road outside my lawn. I leave that east wind to its own devices. I get out some old books, put chestnuts to roast on the bars, ask my *placens uxor* to mull some claret in the etna, with sugar and cinnamon, and loiter in my book-room instead of loitering out of doors. And, looking at the poem wherein Mr. Browning uses that magical phrase, in the edition of 1863, I am carried back a dozen years or so, with numerous recollections. *Tempus edax rerum* is a great saying. Was that the year of Beales and the Park-palings? I know that I was staying at Hatchett's, in Piccadilly, in the famous year of riot, and had, with a friend, to fight my way home through a multitude of roughs. But on reflection, it was later, that ridiculous row, for Lord Palmerston died in 1865, and we were forcing our way home from the club which has set up its quarters in the pleasant house of the cheery descendant of Leofric and Godgifu.

※ ※ ※ ※ *

Why, under the new arrangement, should the Arches Court be held in the library of Lambeth Palace, heretofore the resort of calm students only? To the philosophic mind, the ecclesiastic squabbles are very weak and frivolous: whether a curate at Folkestone did or did not wear a biretta (whatever that may be) seems infinitesimally unimportant. Whoso reads aright the sayings of Christ must see that throughout there is an emphatic protest against mere ceremony. But, as Professor Rogers wittily said, there is nowaday a tendency to make religion a science of symbols, like algebra—*all but the proof.* However, if parsons and parishioners *must* fight—and the new Act clearly exclaims, 'One down, another come on!'—could they not have their fierce contests in some place more fitting than the Lambeth Library, beloved haunt of tranquil, indefatigable students?

* * * * *

I preserve all correspondence that is worth anything, and gum it into the books of its writers or of those whom it concerns. So I have a pleasant series of autograph letters in my books. I mean to leave them to the Plymouth Cottonian Library when I pass into another part of the universe, seeing that Plymouth is my birthplace, and that I have excellent reasons for delighting in the soldierly and erudite family of Cotton.*

Jan. 20.

'The animosities perish; the humanities

* His wife belongs to that family.

are eternal.' I cherish that great saying of Christopher North's, the Sir Launcelot of literature—'The kindest man that every struck with sword.' I am agreeably reminded of it by a passage in Monday's *Western Daily Mercury*, the leading Liberal journal of my native town, the Queen of the West. It is a pleasant comment on that passage in my notes wherein I state that I shall leave my little book-store to the Plymouth and Cottonian Library. It specially refers to the gift books from friends who know that I am fond of literature matured by age. I had mentioned Conrad Gesner's oak-bound Martial of 1544, and the erudite Marcellus Malpighius of 1687. The editor of the *Mercury* and I had many a rapier fight over politics in days half forgotten, so quickly move events; and when Mr. Latimer thus offers his ungauntleted hand in knightly fashion to his old opponent, I gladly do likewise, and thank him heartily for his hope that it will be long before Plymouth gets my little legacy.

Feb. 3.

I have met with a congenial critic, and am happy. If I venture to controvert any of his strictures, it is with diffidence and humility. I am but a Loiterer; he is Aristarchus. He says my egotism is most offensive; that I am always talking about my eating and drinking; that I have positively ventured to solace myself in the wintry weather with roasted chestnuts and mulled claret. 'Because thou art virtuous shall there be no more cakes and ale?' I confess the chestnuts and claret, and heartily wish the latter had been Château Lafitte, which it was not by any means. My kind critic proceeds to object to my having a lawn before my house, but I can assure him it is a very little one. If it were larger I might ask him to come and smoke a cigar upon it; but I feel certain, from his splendid style, that he would dwarf it utterly, as if he were Captain Lemuel Gulliver in the City of Liliput. Further, he remarks that I am in a state of quiet but continuous 'brag' (elegant word!), and that I consider myself 'better off and wiser than the rest of the world!' This is delightful. I confess to being much worse off than most folk — and certainly than my critic, whose style and logic must have made his fortune long ago—for when I manage to make both ends meet, it is by a pretty strong tug at the rope.

But 'wiser'! Nay, this is hard. I am but a Loiterer in the byways of literature. If I may not taste the fount of Parnassus, at least I may hear its immortal murmur. I know well where the wise men go. They haunt the Stock Exchange; they write M.P. after their names; they spend more on a single banquet than I on the modest dinners of a year. I envy them not. The children of this world are wise in their generation. My kind critic, who takes eight copies of this journal, and therefore claims a right to apply a cat-o'-nine-tails to my shoulders, is one of the wise. *O Sapientia!* There were wise men in Greece, and there also were wise men in Gotham: and perchance the great saying of the Lacedæmonian sage might be worth my critic's study.

He has not quite done with me. 'Who is M. C. ?' he writes. 'Pray, pray get rid of him.' Who he is can matter little; and when I began my Loiterings under pleasant auspices I had no notion of a definite signature. I receive so many friendly letters from all parts of the kingdom and from abroad—I get so many books and pamphlets sent me in sole connection with this column, that I can afford to smile at a single ill-natured individual. Still, I think the question has a serious aspect in connexion with journalism. Here is a man who says he takes eight copies of a London newspaper—a drop in the ocean of its circulation—and by reason thereof claims to interfere with its managers and to procure the dismissal of a contributor. Think to what this would lead if such a claim were listened to for a moment.

It may here be remarked that it is quite impossible to write much, or indeed to be in any way much before the public, without annoying somebody. You utter a free opinion, without an idea that it will be taken as a personal insult by some one who thinks differently. I never could understand the temper of mind which induces a man to say, 'You believe the three angles of a triangle are equal to two right angles, and therefore you are a scoundrel and a wretch, and have not yet paid your washerwoman for years.' But there are such delightfully illogical people wandering about :* I charitably hope that my amiable critic is not one of them. And I hereby thank him for his epistle, which amused me greatly as I loitered, with three dogs as comrades, up and down the lawn he so despises. I hope he will not be angry that I laughed just a little.

* * * * *

Turning to Fielding's master-work to verify a quotation—' a little reptile of a critic '—I

---

* All writers for the Press will understand this remark. It is impossible for anyone to ventilate any original opinion or propound any theory without exciting the ire of some 'pestilent knave,' who at once despatches an anonymous letter to the editor of the newspaper, reviling the contributor and praying for his dismissal.—E. Y.

found a case of literary plagiarism which amused me. Hazlitt, in one of his essays, remarks that if you want to know the height of human capacity, you should read Shakespeare; if the lowest depth, you should try his commentators. This has always appeared to me a most epigrammatic antithesis. The idea was manifestly suggested by Fielding, who thus begins a chapter; 'Reader, it is impossible we should know what sort of a person thou wilt be: for perhaps thou mayest be as learned in human nature as Shakespeare himself was, and perhaps thou mayest be no wiser than some of his editors.'

The Vicar of Christchurch, Clifton, ought to read Fielding. Something might be learnt from the military theologians he brings upon the stage. 'And pray, sir,' says the sergeant, 'no offence, I hope; but pray what sort of gentleman is the Devil? For I have heard some of our officers say that there is no such person, and that it is only a trick of the parsons, to prevent their being broke; for if it was publicly known that there was no Devil, the parsons would be of no more use than we are in time of peace.' Let us hope the regimental chaplains knew how to treat these contumacious officers. It certainly does seem strange that in the present day a doubt of the personality of Satan, which the Creeds of the Church do not set forth, should be held to justify excommunication. And it is curious, as Coleridge somewhere remarks, that the modern idea of Satan is got rather from Milton than from the Bible, and that Milton was not a Churchman, nor even an Athanasian, but an Arian of the higher school.

* * * * *

The Americans are doing their utmost to civilise us. They sent us a troop of base-ball players, but that game has not yet superseded cricket. They sent us the skating-rink, and that I believe has been a real benefit to people who must be amused. It should do the young ladies of the day some good; and is a much healthier occupation than gossiping about their acquaintances at five o'clock tea, or than buying things they don't need at a fashionable draper's. But our transatlantic cousins fly

'From grave to gay, from lively to severe,'

and are now enlightening us with the spelling-bee, which is buzzing all through the country. The absurdity of this is, that instead of testing competitors with sound English words, they go to inferior dictionaries for crack-jaw technicalities. Besides, the art of spelling depends on etymology, and the competitor ought to give his reason for his reply. To spell without reason is parrot work: it is like doing sums in arithmetic without knowing the principles. Take the two words *Augur* and *Auger*, pronounced alike. It would be some exercise in language if candidates were asked why they are spelt differently. The *au* in the former means a bird, in the latter a centre; to prove these points would show some knowledge. The *ger* in the carpenter's tool is from *gar*, to bore; the *gur* in the Roman diviner is from an old root, meaning to stare. The one is bird-starer; the other centre-borer. But the patrons of spelling-bees know none of these things. They are ultra-crepidarian, as Southey has it. A big bad dictionary is their final authority. So they arrive at what has been called a floccinaucical nihilipitification—which words let them spell and digest.

Feb. 24.

A Bristol correspondent asks me whether it is true that the nightingale is never heard in Devonshire. I certainly have not heard its unmistakable note in that county. Patterson ('Zoology,' ii. 347) says that 'it does not appear to frequent Cornwall or Wales; it is not found more than five miles north of York, and is consequently absent from Scotland and the neighbouring islands; and it is altogether unknown in Ireland.' The cock nightingales reach England from the south in April, usually a fortnight before the hens: this interval is the time of their most joyous song. Evidently they only take to a strip of country which lies, roughly speaking, between about 50° 30′ and 54°.

March 2.

I have this week voted by ballot for the first time in my life. I cannot say I like it. The ballot may be a necessity in clubs, very likely—that is a point on which I express no opinion; but in political voting it is, in my judgment, most humiliating. A gentleman who had the same duty to perform told me that when he went through the process of secret voting he felt 'a dreadful sneak.' That phrase tersely describes the feeling of an Englishman, accustomed to a fair and open encounter, when compelled to vote in the dark, and to conceal the name of the man he votes for. It seems impossible that a system can last which is so abhorrent to all the manlier instincts of our strong and fearless race.

March 9.

One meets with odd experiences in literary matters. Once upon a time, to use the good old-fashioned story-opening phrase, I was asked by the projector of an inchoant and rather incoherent periodical to produce an essay on 'The Rationale of Religious Scepticism.' Well, that is a topic which might be treated from many points of view; and the diagnosis of a purely rational sceptic would, I take it, be rather interesting. A sceptic, primarily, means a person who examines. However, I asked my editor for further instructions, and he wrote to me thus: 'I say most boldly, after investigating the question closely on scientific principles, that it cannot be known whether there is or is not a God. ['That *I* cannot know,' is what he should say.] I do not pretend to know so much as some people who perchance have travelled the heavens and espied something (as they say) which they term God. I would like to ask these people how they know that the same God is in existence which [*sic*] they affirm created the world, for it does not follow *that*, if we find a watch going, *that* therefore the maker is living.' Poor Paley! He never expected to have his well-known illustration twisted round in that fashion. I did not write that essay, though it certainly occurred to me that the thing might have been done in an ironical vein, which I am sure that sapient editor would not have detected.

March 23.

Snow on the vernal equinox, with white violets in full bloom. Just seven days later than I noted it six years ago. The seasons do not improve. The old-fashioned summers, when there was

'A strange superfluous glory in the air,'

are memories of the past. When did we last sit on the lawn, day after day, glad of the shadow of full-foliaged trees, stimulated by Apollo's actinic shafts? It seems ages ago. Is Ἥλιος ἄναξ growing weary? Does Hertha feel a flagging energy? I fancy not. This is a world of cycles, and periods of fine and bad weather alternate on much the same principle as that which produces Tory and Whig ministries, Ritualism and Rationalism, striped petticoats and crinoline, good and bad luck at cards. I am an optimist. The longer my ill-luck lasts, the more assured am I of a run of good luck. Who waits, wins. When I am ill I habitually look forward to getting well, and

I do it. Some fellows no sooner feel a pain in their little finger than they proclaim their intention to die, and very often fulfil that intention. Of course it is absurd for snow to be persistently falling on the 20th of March; but when I find Gilbert White recording snow late in April, and ice as thick as a crown-piece on the 7th of June, 1787, I conclude that our grandfathers were as badly off as we. And, through the calmly-falling snow, which is rapidly whitening the yews and hollies and laurels, I have a vision of the same lawn in July, when the limes now leafless will be sunproof, and the turf now snow-covered will be greener than emerald, softer than velvet. There is a missel-thrush singing riotously through the wild weather; for he is wooing his mate, and the bitter air cannot freeze his lyric force; in July he will be silent, save for sometimes a twitter in morning and evening twilight. Surely he foresees summer, or he could not sing so rarely.

March 30.

All through the wintry weather—from quite

the beginning of February—a missel-thrush has been cheering us by continual song. He begins at five in the morning: he sings till seven at night. He has really made me feel as 'jolly as a sandboy' (the small shrimp so called, that frisks in the maddest way about the sands) on days almost suicidal. But to-day, turning over Gilbert White, I am reminded that the missel-thrush 'is called in Hampshire and Sussex the storm-cock, because his song is supposed to forbode windy wet weather.' Storm-cock, indeed! So my musical friend up in the naked lime-boughs, singing madly from before sunrise to after sunset, only pausing to descend and tug a luckless worm out of the turf, *you* are a herald of wind and snow, are you? And I have all this while been admiring your cheerfulness in adverse weather. One learns a little every day.

April 1.

Spring at last. Why, we shall be having the swallow soon. Verily, it is hard to believe, after the long, keen winter through which we have passed. It has been often said—I know not by whom said first—that we enjoy autumn most in our youth and spring in our age. The reason is reasonable enough—namely, that as you grow older the melancholy of autumn grows more oppressive. I must have been born old.* I always loved spring for its promise of the royal summer. It is the herald of the King of the Year. Its violets fearless of snow, and wind-blown daffodils which gave Wordsworth his only knowledge of odour,† and celandine that shines with glossy gold at the elm-tree root, are the banners of the vanguard. Trumpet of thrush and blackbird, fife of robin and wren, prepare us for the cuckoo, untirable bugler, and for the divine chorus of nightingales that will sing King Summer to sleep behind the crimson curtains of sunset. Yes: I have always liked Spring; and this year I like it all the more, because that rebel Winter has been so hard to kill.

* It was perhaps rather the other way, that he never grew old. To the last he was boyish in manner and young in spirit.—F. C.

† Wordsworth is said to have been without the sense of smell: but that he once caught the perfume of daffodils in passing a field of them.—F. C.

* * * * *

Mr. Otto Trevelyan's memoir of Macaulay must be a most readable book, judging from reviews. But what a marvellous mind Macaulay had! Few people could have endured the curse of such a stupendous memory. I should be sorry to remember all the Senior Wranglers of Cambridge, or all the Archbishops of Canterbury, or a hundred other similar things which Macaulay had stowed away in his many pigeon-holed brain. Such a memory must lessen originality. However, we owe Macaulay much—essays and a history which young readers delight in, but which are too sweet for the mature palate—a style whose masterly monotony has degenerated into heavy sameness in the hands of modern journalists—and the spectacle of one man who went directly counter to Dr. Johnson's famous saying, and believed that all political virtue resided with the Whigs.

* * * * *

Mr. Lowe has again been singing the praises of the Civil Engineers. The engineer is an important entity, but he is not precisely the ruler of the world; and when Mr. Lowe tells me it is all Plato's fault that the Roman empire came to grief, I am disposed to be thankful to Plato. The Roman empire had lasted quite long enough when its time came to be shattered. Mr. Lowe may fool the engineers to the top of their bent; but if this realm of England ever sinks to the godless and soulless depth which had been reached by the empire he regrets, not all the great engineers in the world will save it from being hurled into the abyss. The final forces of life are not mechanical, but spiritual. Alaric and Attila were thunderbolts of God, which descended on a pestilent, putrescent phase of society. It is odd to see so progressive a thinker as the member for the University of London bemoaning the destruction of the greatest political incubus that ever stayed the forward movement of men.

* * * * *

Modern medical writers are perpetually urging people not to drink too much, and not to take too much exercise. Both warnings are good, without doubt; yet I cannot believe that alcohol is to be regarded, as some of these earnest preachers say, as the primal source of all human maladies; nor am I disposed to think that a vigorous race like the English will readily be induced to resign their favourite sports because they are told that they shorten life. The torpid life of a reptile is not enviable; existence really should be measured rather by ideas and sensations than by moments. We live a rapid, nervous life, and the fashionable doctors take advantage of it and try to frighten us. Drink nothing. Walk, and ride, and row, as little as possible. Never sit up late. Never allow anything to interfere with the equanimity of your temper. Such are the wise sayings of our neoteric sages. I am inclined to add—Never marry, lest your wife should worry you to death, and lest the race of fools should increase.

Well, it is April Fool's Day. Thus I wrote, on the 1st of April—I wonder how many years ago—to a sweetheart of mine:

Comes April, her white fingers wet with flowers,
And we might well enjoy her sunny showers,
If the malignant Fate which o'er us rules
    Did not bring April Fools.

Fools who will whisper, you and I together
Ought not to wander in the sweet spring weather,
For I'm a boy and you're a girl, and so
    'Tis very wrong, you know.

To hunt for violets in meadows fair
Till April rains her diamonds on your hair,
Is really such a silly girlish fashion,
    It puts them in a passion.

Youth's joy must have its grim concomitants,
Its sulky sisters and its maiden aunts.
Well, let them scowl at us, and keep their rules—
    We won't be April Fools.

                April 6.

Undergraduates now appear to outdo the past follies of princes. We are authentically informed that the Prince Regent and the Duke of York were wont to drive from London to Brighton a tandem of three—no very princely amusement. A few days ago I saw a tandem of four pull up at a wayside inn, the nominal driver being a young Oxford man, but the real manager of the reins a boozy, red-faced fellow, with the dirtiest white hat I ever saw encircled by a black hat-band, who offered to bet the bystanders 500 to 1 that he could drive more horses in a line than any man in England. To drive such wretched hacks as those he had in hand was not at all a brilliant achievement. Young Oxford, sitting beside that vulgar fellow, behind that string of worn-out screws, and delighting in the contemptuous applause of barmaids and stablemen, was to me, who believe in the vast importance of our English Universities, not at all a pleasant sight. Mr. Matthew Arnold wittily applies to Oxford a line of 'Childe Harold':

'There are our young barbarians, all at play.'

Well, when their play takes no worse form than boating or cricket, by all means let them have a fair share of it; but when I see an Oxford man driven behind four hacks by an unfragrant Yahoo of the stables, and himself feebly blowing a long horn, I am moved to pity for that youth's imbecile eccentricity.

April 13.

When a man of some mark is dead, is it

quite the right thing that anyone who pleases, without authority from his family or representatives—without perhaps any special knowledge of him, should be at liberty to write his life? The case of Mr. Hawker, of Morwenstow, an excellent but eccentric clergyman, and a minor poet of about the third or fourth magnitude, is very much to the point. Two memoirs of this unlucky gentleman were issued—one by Dr. Lee, the other by Mr. Baring-Gould. The former is, I believe, fair enough; but Mr. Gould's memoir, which he tells us is 'undergoing revision,' seems full of atrocious and incredible stories about the deceased clergyman. The *Athenæum* justly remarked that, if certain stories told by the biographer were true, Mr. Hawker was an unfit subject for biography. No man can be much before the world without suffering from the circulation of gossip, which George Eliot describes as 'a sort of smoke that comes from the dirty tobacco-pipes of those who diffuse it, and that proves nothing but the bad taste of the smoker.' Most men of unusual power have peculiarities which the vulgar folk cannot understand: whence there rises around them a rank growth of myth. Now if any biographic scandal-vendor may take up rumours and stories which flutter about a man of genius, and print them to please morbid tastes, the result will be unpleasant. The idea of it 'adds a terror to death.' The greater the scandals the more spicy the memoir; and there are always people hugely delighted at the revelation that men of higher intellect than their own have their feeble points. A certain term of years should pass before anyone might write a man's life without the consent of his literary executor or of his family. *For my part, I mean to leave as a legacy to any unauthorised biographer the fiercest malediction I can concoct, after careful study of the literature of anathemas.**

May 4.

Classical illustration in the modern novel is

---

* Mortimer Collins was himself unfortunate in having an unauthorised biographer in the writer of certain articles in a monthly magazine; but the writer had probably not seen these words.—F. C.

very charming, seeing that the modern novel is too often written by gentlemen (and ladies) with a fine contempt for the classics—a contempt only surpassed by their ignorance. In an amusing novel by two or more authors, contributed to an always amusing and arrogant contemporary, I find a charming bit of classicism. The idea is, what you might do if you had any amount of money, and here is one possibility :

'You could take the journey to Asia Minor, your dream of forty years, and sketch the temples still standing, roofed and perfect, unvisited since the last stragglers of the last crusading army died of famine on the steps, scoffing with their latest breath at the desecrated altar. Their bones lay mouldering in front of the marble columns—silent monuments of a wasted enthusiasm—while the fleshless fingers pointed as if in scorn in the direction of Jerusalem. They have been dust this many a year. Dust blown about the fields ; manure for the crops which the peasant raises in luxuriance by scratching the soil. But the temples stand still, sacred yet to the memory of Mother Earth, the manybreasted goddess of the Ephesians.'

I read this with much interest. Those 'fleshless fingers' are fine. 'Dust blown about the fields' is a great touch. I smelt pulverised crusader in my nostrils, and I sneezed in-

Thoughts in my Garden. 289

tensely. But I was pulled up rather by 'the many-breasted goddess of the Ephesians.' What a scandal about our virgin Artemis, that Ephesus was so proud of as an immaculate goddess! Could it be a mistake? Had a perverse printer put *Ephesians* instead of *Eleusinians*? Impossible: since 'many-breasted' is an epithet unmistakable, and Asia Minor is mentioned just above. So we are forced to the inference that these tremendously classical novelists (for 'tis a duet) don't know Ephesus from Eleusis, or Demeter from Artemis. Doubtless they went to some school where the birch-rod was disestablished. This being so, why should they attempt to be classical? The young ladies who read novels don't want to be sent to their weary old 'Mangnall's Questions' to look up 'Ephesus' in search of its divinity. The dears have their Bibles, and know what is the value of a wise town clerk on an emergency.

* * * * *

May is bringing us the sunshine and flowers and birds which in years long past we used to expect in April. Lilacs are trying to burst into bloom, nightingales are in full song, and the cuckoo :

> ' No bird, but an invisible thing,
> A voice, a mystery '—

is heard in a myriad coppices. Has there really been a recession of the seasons, so that summer comes later year after year? To common observers it would appear so; and the philosophers are so occupied with high matters, not very interesting to ordinary mortals, that they can spare no thought for meteorology. Admiral Fitzroy and Lieutenant Saxby both showed that meteoric mysteries are not utterly beyond the ken of mankind: but nobody treads in their steps, and we take the weather as it comes, without asking why. Last year I heard the nightingale on March 24, the cuckoo on April 12; this year they were much later. Now, it is impossible to doubt that the birds forecast changes of weather, and are guided by them in their migrations; and what the instinct of birds can do ought not to be wholly beyond the reason of man.

If Messrs. Huxley and Tyndall could only conquer meteorology enough to tell the ladies each year when it is safe to put on spring dresses, they would earn considerable gratitude.

May 6.

Mr. Grantley Berkeley gives me permission to tell one of the best (if not the very best) stories of dog intelligence I ever heard. Its hero, Jack, has killed some hundreds of rats. One afternoon there came upon the lawn at Alderney Manor a giant house rat: Mr Berkeley shot him from the window, and little Jack ran him down in the shrubbery, and brought him in triumphantly—a rat almost as big as himself. But, from having to seize the monster among the laurels, Jack, for the first time in his rat-killing career, got bitten—twice, under the eye. Rats' bites are venomous, probably because rats are scavengers, and feed on carrion and other putrid matter. The doctor ordered calomel to be blown into Jack's eye two or three times a day. The only quill available was a toothpick, and with this his master performed the operation. Now comes the fun of the thing. Mr. Grantley Berkeley was one day killing time by raking some new-laid gravel on his carriage-drive, when he noticed Jack walk out of the dining-room in a dignified way, with an odd expression in his face. Jack looked at his master, but his master would not appear to see him. Thereon the little dog walked solemnly along the drive, found a place which he deemed suitable for funereal purposes, scratched a hole, and *buried that toothpick.* This done, he returned with an easy mind. If calomel were again to be blown into his eye, at any rate his master would have to find another toothpick. Who shall say that dogs do not reason? That Jack associated his ocular trouble with the toothpick, rather than with the calomel blown through it, merely shows that he was as shortsighted as we mortals who boast articulate speech and formal logic. Jack ought, of course, to have gone further back still, and discovered that the calomel was administered for his good, and been grateful to the toothpick. But are human beings grateful to their toothpicks in like conditions? I am promised a son of Jack's, as yet unborn, and I hope he will be as brave and friendly and clever as his sire.

I write this somewhat after midnight, in the centre—the very core—of London.* The mighty heart of the world's greatest City is lying still. I suppose the guardsmen who take charge of the Bank of England, whose roof I see from my bedroom window, have finished dinner.

* * * * *

Monday morning, and the Seventy-seventh Regiment (which Picton commanded at Waterloo) are at the door of the Mansion House with their tattered colours, to be placed in St. Paul's over Noble's famous monument to the officers and men (nearly six hundred) who died in the Crimean campaign. Colonel

---

* Mortimer Collins was on a visit to the Lord Mayor (Alderman Cotton) at the Mansion House.—F. C.

Kent—on a charger that has been twice to India, once to Australia, and that Colonel Stratton rode through the Crimean war—presented the colours to the Lord Mayor. That royal rag! The mad whirl of many battles has worn it to threads; and now, in the calm Cathedral of London, it will slowly drop to dust. War and peace are friends. If the gallant Seventy-seventh had not been willing to die for the realm, there would be no Lord Mayor of London, no calm Cathedral of St. Paul. When Colonel Kent and the Lord Mayor had exchanged speeches (excellent good on both sides), the regiment marched to St. Paul's, and the colours were solemnly presented. The Dean, receiving them, laid them on the altar of God; then, after fit ceremony, they were placed above the monument to those brave brothers of ours who died for England. Never have I been more impressed by any solemnity. When I saw those torn flags of many victories placed upon the shrine of everlasting peace, I wished to be young again, that I might choose another vocation, and use the sword rather than the pen in defence of religion and loyalty.

May 25.

At a pleasant Berkshire mansion the other day I made the acquaintance of a pair of tame emus. They seem harmless enough, but are apparently fond of a practical joke. At first they were allowed to wander on the lawn at the entrance; but whenever the carriage drove up, and the footman jumped rapidly down to open the door, the emus at once ran after him and seized his hat. In consequence of this humorous habit, they have been confined to a turfed enclosure, where they receive human visitors with great courtesy. Last year the hen laid six eggs. These are of a mottled dark green, extremely beautiful; and the shell is so thick that one, mounted in silver, has been made into an elegant drinking-cup. As the hen is a very clean feeder, I suspect the eggs are good to eat, but the experiment has not in this case been tried. Ostrich eggs in aspic are extremely good, *experto crede;* I really cannot see why those of the emu should not be worth the epicure's attention.

The other day I found a young man shooting at small birds close to the high-road, and thereby breaking two Acts of Parliament at once. If, as is likely enough, he had no gun license, he was of course breaking three. When I warned him that it was a matter for the police, he said, in a supercilious way, that he shot birds 'for artistic and scientific purposes.' Verily, I thought, the schoolmaster is abroad. This youth with the gun is artist and scientist; I, knowing it not, have treated him irreverently. Juvenal's saying, *Maxima debetur puero reverentia*, assumes a new meaning now that youth has grown so singularly sapient. However, as I knew where this precocious personage was to be found, I requested the Superintendent of Police (who probably will care little for his art and science) to administer a warning.

June 22.

I was talking the other day to a young lady who had been fascinated by a prose translation of the great Homeric Hymn to Demeter, published in a recent number of the *Cornhill Magazine*. I have not seen the translation, and cannot therefore say whether it is good, bad, or indifferent. The hymn itself, by its marvellous poetry, and its real religious feeling, is unique among the products of the Greek mind; it belongs to the time when Homer had not been crystallised by the dramatists. The divine legends of Delos and Cythera had at least a half belief. Demeter, the Earth Mother, was a mighty fact, whose influence lasted to the days when the Athenian women swore 'by the two Goddesses'—Demeter and Persephoneia—Earth and the produce of Earth. I could not help wishing, when my fair friend asked me for information about this great Homeric hymn, that the ladies of to-day got as good an education as if they had lived in Tudor times. What did poor Princess Elizabeth, a prisoner at Bisham Abbey, uncertain whether she should save her neck, do to pass the time? There were no daily papers. The three volume novel had not been invented.

Mr. Swinburne was unborn—and so was Mr. Shakespeare. What could she do, in that pleasant, airy chamber which was her reception-room, and which Mr. George Vansittart maintains in such charming order? Do! why read Greek. And so she did; and if you were to suggest such solace to the intellectual young lady of the present day, I wonder what she would say to you. You would have an Alpha of amazement, a Delta of tears, an Iota of common sense, an Omega of curt dismissal. Yet I should like ladies to learn Greek.

Before Latin? Most assuredly. Greek is a human language; Latin (except in Catullus the inimitable) is merely a *man's* language. As a man's language for strong virile work, it can never have equal. Its *period* could only have been invented by the grave, determined Conquerors of the World. It has established itself as the definite and indestructible language of all scholars, of all inscriptions. It is the very algebra of language, and has taken form more from Cicero and Cæsar and Horace than from Catullus and Ovid. I like Latin, I must say;

but I don't consider it a lady's language. Greek is. Sappho wrote in it; and, though according to the best evidence she was rather a naughty, passionate young creature, her few words are indestructible, immortal. The naughty young creatures of to-day, who gush into three volume novels, are not at all immortal. They have no echo of

Ποικιλόθρον', ἀθανάτ' Ἀφροδίτα.

Mr. Thorold Rogers publishes a volume of 'Epistles, Satires and Epigrams,' which is really very enjoyable. One preliminary objection. Mr. Rogers simply paraphrases Horace and Juvenal, applying them to this present time. The first thing that occurs to the reader is that the present time ought to have its own native satire—that is to say, if satire, in poetic form, is at all necessary. I do not think it is. With the press wide awake to all the weaknesses of the time, I doubt whether the poet might not find better employment than lashing pachydermatous fools. Had there been a dozen daily papers in Rome, Horace would not have written leaders in Alcaic verse, and Juvenal would never have been driven to his magnificent outburst of wrath. However, Mr. Rogers does remarkably well what has been done a great many times before. He is a bit of a Radical, and it would do him good to study the works of a more thorough Republican than himself —a man of whom Warwickshire should be almost as proud as of Shakespeare—Walter Savage Landor. Landor puts into the mouth of Alfieri, in the too seldom read 'Imaginary Conversations,' this great saying: 'A poet cannot be an atheist; a gentleman cannot be a leveller.' I leave that text for anyone who thinks he understands it to preach upon. Those are readiest to preach who are slowest to understand.

July, 1876.

Professor Sydney Colvin, in the always suggestive magazine from which I took this stray quotation, has some noticeable words on the waste of literary power in periodical writing. He is replying to Mr. Brodrick: 'That superiority of English writing in newspapers and magazines which Mr. Brodrick extols, and concerning which, dared he "unlock the secrets of journalism," he would evidently furnish still more impressive disclosures—that superiority certainly exists, but at what cost? At the cost, surely, of superiority in serious literature, and especially in the literature of learning. The amount of force which is frittered in this ephemeral work, and might have gone to produce work not ephemeral, is immense. It is, I think, one of the great wastes of a wasteful generation. We are all of us sufferers by the waste. A hundred newspaper and magazine articles, in which the best ideas are tossed out incomplete, leave us where they found us; a single book, in which a moderately good idea is worked out to completion, carries us a step onwards.' This is a half-truth of Professor Colvin's. I confess, when I look through the file of *Adversaria*, I think what a *magnum opus* it ought to be. But I chance to know that a few of my words in this desultory column have been read with pleasure by men of genius, and

that also they have suggested useful ideas
to aspirant young folk. So I plod quietly
along this winding, shady, flower-fenced lane
of literature, leaving lofty charioteers to
drive their four-in-hand on the high road
of fame.*

* The greater part of these notes have been taken from a
newspaper column, which Mortimer Collins wrote from
week to week for ten years, called 'Adversaria,' and signed
'Cæcilius.' It was the only place in print where he felt
that he could speak his mind, for the learned and kindly
editor, Mr. Kydd, thoroughly appreciated him, and laid no
restriction on him. The paper was not a widely circulated
one, but many clever men read this column of *Adversaria*
from week to week with pleasure. It brought the writer
much correspondence, chiefly of a pleasant sort; but it also
brought anonymous letters from churlish folk who complained that Mortimer was egotistical, and always writing of
himself and his surroundings. Whatever blame may attach
to a man for egotism during his lifetime, there is a satisfaction in reading his thoughts and feelings after his death,
if he has made his mark in the world. The admirers of
Mortimer Collins are perhaps not very numerous—though
they are increasing; but they will, with me, thank the
editor who gave him the opportunity of making this record
of the last few years of his life—years which brought the
'philosophic mind' without destroying the poetic.

As his wife, I may be considered too partial a judge; but
I do not claim greatness for my husband, I simply place
him before the public as a large-hearted, lovable man, who
by his life and conversation could bestow happiness on all
around him, and by his writings can still please many

thousands. In his own home he was truly a hero; and since his death it has been some consolation to me to know that his name is cherished in many households where he is known only by his writings. It must always be remembered that he was at a disadvantage because he was struggling with poverty; but he struggled nobly and bravely, and did not murmur. The concluding words of this volume were written shortly before his death, and seem to be, as it were, a review of his life. He was content, as he said, to 'plod quietly along the winding, shady, flower-fenced lane of literature;' and to us who knew him it is, verily, a flower-fenced lane.—F. C.

THE END.

BILLING AND SONS, PRINTERS AND ELECTROTYPERS, GUILDFORD.

S. & H.

www.ingramcontent.com/pod-product-compliance
Lightning Source LLC
Chambersburg PA
CBHW022028240426
43667CB00042B/1243